# Children Of The Greys

## Bret Oldham

Foreword by **Dr. R. Leo Sprinkle, Ph.D.**

**with Contributions by**

**Kathleen Mardeen, Brad Stieger,
Brent Raynes and Sandy Nichols**

Edited by **Brent Raynes**

Cover art and book sketches

Copyright © 2013 Jeffrey Oldham

**Jeffrey Oldham**

www.OldhamArt.com

Copyright © 2013 Bret Oldham

Published by

House of Halo

Murfreesboro, TN. U.S.A.

ISBN: 978-0-9891031-3-8

# About The Author
## Bret Oldham

**B**ret Oldham has been researching and investigating the paranormal since his teen years. Together with his wife Gina, they are Halo Paranormal and are based out of Murfreesboro, Tennessee. Their research encompasses a wide spectrum of the paranormal including Ghosts, UFO's and Cryptozoology. They have been featured on numerous radio shows, magazine and newspaper articles, Internet TV, local and national TV in the USA, New Zealand and Europe. Television appearances include being the featured guests on the prime time television program "The New Files" in Bulgaria, two episodes of, "My Ghost Story", on the Bio Channel, an episode on alien abductions, which features one of Bret's abduction events from this book; for a new show called, "Monsters and Mysteries In America" on the Destination America channel, for the Discovery network, and the nationally televised CBC television show "The Conspiracy Show" in Canada, among others.

Bret and Gina contributed two articles to the book, "Real Ghosts, Restless Spirits and Haunted Places" by renown author Brad Steiger. Bret contributed a chapter on "Spirit Communication" for the book,

"Mystery US Universe, Origins and Destiny". Bret has contributed articles to Bigfoot newsletters and has interviewed such UFO luminaries as Travis Walton and John Lear which were first published by Alternate Perceptions magazine and later picked up worldwide. Bret is also the author of, "Ghost Stories Of Las Vegas".

Contact info -

www.haloparanormal1@hotmail.com
www.facebook.com/haloparanormal
www.childrenofthegreys.com

# Table Of Contents

# Acknowledgements

It took years for me to get the courage to come forth with my story and write the contents of this book. It was a difficult and long process, and I couldn't have done it without the help, guidance and encouragement of my family, friends and my colleagues in the UFO field.

First and foremost I want to thank my wonderful wife Gina for all the years of love and understanding. It was Gina who first urged me to begin writing this book. It is often not easy to live with those of us who have had these experiences but through it all she has been a pillar of strength and support along this journey and for that I am eternally grateful.

I would like to express my heartfelt gratitude to all my amazing contributors, Sandy Nichols, Brent Raynes, Brad Steiger, and Kathleen Marden, whose insight and knowledge of the alien abduction phenomena is invaluable. I am humbled and honored that each of you were gracious enough to be a part of this book. I have the utmost respect for all of you, your work, and all you have done to bring awareness and understanding of this often controversial subject to the masses.

I would also like to thank my good friend Sandy Nichols for his words of encouragement for me when I first started thinking about revealing to the public this long held secret of my alien abductions; for his no holds barred advice for what to expect from going public and in writing this book.

To my brother Jeffrey Oldham for lending his amazing art talent which brought to life such close approximations to the events I experienced. The hybrid child he created on my cover is stunning and as close to the real thing as I have ever seen. I am in awe!

I would like to express a very sincere thank you to Dr. R. Leo Sprinkle PH.D for writing such a wonderful forward. Your work and life are an inspiration. Your concern and caring for those of us who live with these experiences is unparalleled. I am very proud to have you be a part of "Children Of The Greys".

I owe a deep debt of gratitude to my good friend Brent Raynes who has been instrumental in helping bring this book to see the light of day. His advice, suggestions, editing and devotion of his valuable time are appreciated more than words can say.

And last but certainly not least, I would like to thank those in my family who have supported me through it all especially my Mother Loretta, my brother Jeffrey, my daughter Haley, and my aunt and uncle, Annette and Dennis. Thank you all for your continued support, understanding, love and unwavering belief in me.

# Foreword

## By Dr. R. Leo Sprinkle, Ph.D.

*Dr. R. Leo Sprinkle is legendary pioneer of UFO contactee research and reincarnation. He demonstrates this extensive knowledge in his book "Soul Samples", where he presents information gathered from hundreds of hypnosis clients and participants in psychological studies.*

*He began his career in psychology with the idea of being a conventional, practicing "scientist" in the traditional sense. However, two close encounters with UFOs shattered Dr. Sprinkle's conventional reality and shifted his direction in life. After the second incident experienced with his wife, he knew that he had to investigate the UFO phenomena, and that it would be a lonely task.*

*Dr. Sprinkle began his investigations from the conventional viewpoint, but found he was unable to make further progress until he became aware of—and accepted— the psychical aspects of UFO phenomena. He became more and more skeptical—ironically not of the reality of "flying saucers," but of the concept of "reality" as defined and developed by the current scientific community.*

*As a pioneer in the UFO field, Dr. Sprinkle was in the limelight early on and participated in many regional and national television programs, including ABC-TV (That's Incredible) and NBC-TV (Tom Snyder, Tomorrow Show) and NBC's UFOs: Fact or Fantasy. He has appeared on many panels with scientists such as J.Allen Hynek and Carl Sagan. Ruth Montgomery included a chapter on Sprinkle's activities in her 1985 book, Aliens Among Us. He has been invited to speak at several international conferences and numerous other meetings and conferences.*

*With his pioneering view of the role contactees played within the UFO/ET phenomena, he started the first UFO Investigation Conference for "contactees" held on the campus of the University of Wyoming.*

*Dr. Sprinkle received his Ph.D. in Counseling Psychology from the University of Missouri in 1961. He completed his BA & MPS at the University of Colorado in 1952 and 1956 respectively. Dr. Sprinkle was a Professor of Counseling Services at the University of Wyoming and for the last 13 years of his career he served as the Director of Counseling Services.*

*Currently, he is Professor Emeritus of Counseling Services at the University of Wyoming and a Counseling Psychologist in Laramie, Wyoming. He is nationally certified and licensed and a Registrant of Counsel for the National Register of Health Service Providers.*

*Additionally Dr. Sprinkle is a member of several Professional Organizations, including the American Association for the Advancement of Science, the American Association for Counseling, and the Association for Past-Life Research and Therapies.*

*His publications include several encyclopedia entries, a half dozen book chapters, and approximately 50 published articles on the following topics: counseling theory and practice; ESP; hypnosis; reincarnation; and UFO research. Some of his articles include: Personal Characteristics of UFO Witnesses; University of Wyoming, 1986; Hypnotic and Psychic Implications in the Investigation of UFO Reports, With C.E. Lorenzen and J. Lorenzen;*

*Encounters with UFO Occupants, New York: Berkley Press; What are the Implications of UFO Experiences? Journal for UFO Studies, 1, No. 1.*

I am both pained and pleased to write an introduction to this book, I am pained to learn of the deep trauma that the Author has experienced. However, I am pleased to learn that the Author, Bret Oldham is accepting of reincarnation as a process for Human Development. Bret was supportive and encouraging when I told him that I was willing to write this Foreword, as long as I could provide another version of what can be called "The Alien Agenda."

In 1961, I joined NICAP (National Investigations Committee on Ariel Phenomena). In 1962, I joined APRO (Ariel Phenomena Research Organization), working with Jim and Coral Lorenzen, and their consultants, Dr. Jim Harder, Ph.D., and Dr. Frank Salisbury, Ph.D. In those days, the game was simple: In regard to flying saucers, players were Skeptics or Believers.

In fact, in 1966, I participated in two TV programs in New York City; one program, with astronomers Dr. J. Allen Hynek, Ph.D., and Dr. Howard Menzel, Ph.D., and others, was called "Flying Saucers: Fact or Fiction?" The other program, with astronomer, Dr. Carl Sagan, Ph.D., and physicist, Dr. Jim McDonald, Ph.D., and others were interviewing Betty and Barney Hill, about their 1961 encounter with a strange craft and its occupants.

Gradually, the game changed from Skeptics and Believers to a more complex game: Those persons called Skeptics sometimes turned out to be Debunkers. Those of us who were called Believers sometimes turned out to be Knowers: We had experienced encounters with Entities, on board space craft and we described our interactions with these Entities.

Throughout Human History, there have been many legends, in various cultures and traditions, about the "Gods." Many interpretations have been provided about the meaning of angels, demons, Jinn's, Elohim, Star People, et. al.

The Author describes his experiences with some Greys that indicate a range of concerns; Psychic Phenomena; Human Emotions; Human Sexuality; Human Reproduction; and Human Spirituality.

The important question, from our Human viewpoint, is the question of purpose. What are the motives of Extraterrestrial interactions with us Humans? There are various answers to the questions, depending on who is perceived as an "expert" in reviewing and interpreting those experiences.

Some experts, e.g., Dr. David Jacobs, Ph.D., view ETs as Invaders. Some experts, e.g., Budd Hopkins (now deceased) view ETs as Intruders. Some experts, e.g., Dr. Kenneth Ring, Ph.D., view ETs as Instructors. Some experts, e.g., Dr. James W. Deardorff, Ph.D., view ETs as Initiators. Dr. Deardorff (Professor of Atmospheric Sciences and a New Testament Scholar) has written Celestial Teachings, and other books about the connection of ETs and the teachings of Jesus, including reincarnation. Ida Kannenberg (now deceased), and others, have written about channeled messages from ETs and Extra Dimensional Entities.

The basic scenario of ETs as Good Guy/Bad Guy (some ETs as Helpful and some ETs as Hurtful to Humans) has shifted to include another scenario: Good Cop/Bad Cop. In this scenario, the ETs could be perceived as Galactic Guardians, checking on Earthlings, who are the Bad Guys: polluting the Planet; killing animal and plant species; oppressing women and children; stockpiling nuclear weapons; taking weapons out into space; etc. In this scenario, ETs could be viewed as Mentors (or Tormentors) who are testing the knowledge and the morality of Humans. Humans could be viewed as "trainees" who are being prepared to become Cosmic Citizens and interacting with other civilization throughout the Galaxy.

If the Reader chooses, He or She can view this book as an "initiation" for the Author, Bret Oldham, he has returned from his Hero's Journey: "removed" from Society by his childhood encounters with ETs; experiencing fearful and traumatic reactions; challenged and tested by his interactions with Grey Mentors (or Tormentors); revealing his strength and courage by openly talking about his "journey"; and now sharing his knowledge with others around him. Thus, this model of Star People is similar to the Model of Reality: Nature/Body/Mind/Soul: the craft (Nature); the crew (Body); the messengers (Mind); the message (Soul).

And what is the message? As Bret is told by a tall Grey; we are all one with the one who is all. In this scenario, various groups of

ETs (not only the Greys) are seen as actors and actresses in a "theatre." They are putting on a show: The UFO/ET Display. The show (Cosmic Consciousness Conditioning) can be described as a MIRROR. The ET Mirror (or Ink Blot Test in the Sky) reflects back to us who we are, not who they are.

Thus, ETs can be viewed as evil and threatening, or as alien and strange, or as friends and family, depending upon the viewer's level of spirituality. This model of the ET Agenda, provides questions for our Planetary Agenda: Are we Humans ready to learn more about our own Emotions? Our sexuality? Our Psychic Abilities? Our Origins? Our readiness for "free" energy? Our greed and violence? If Energy, not oil, gas, coal, nuclear fission, is available, could we end wars and feed, clothe, shelter, educate, and provide medical assistance to every man, woman, and child on the Planet? (When I spoke to a friend about this vision, he responded: "Leo, is that Socialism?" Or Communism?" I replied: "Or Christianity? "

The Author, Bret Oldham, has set the stage for the next act in Human/ET interactions. We have come from the Stars, and now we are poised to return to the Stars.

Perhaps, when Disclosure of the ET presence is announced, and new energy systems are revealed, we shall have the opportunity to communicate openly with representatives of the Galactic Federation, and to learn their perspective of Human History and our potential to become Cosmic Citizens.

Meanwhile, I commend Bret Oldham for his courage, curiosity, and compassion in sharing his experiences and his knowledge.

May we all share Love & Light

R. Leo Sprinkle, Ph.D.,
Professor Emeritus, Counseling Services, University of Wyoming.

# Chapter 1.

# Innocence Lost

The farmland of Southern Illinois seems like a safe place to a young child. Small rural towns dot the countryside. Two lane highways lead to gravel roads that lead to dirt roads. The flat fertile land is filled with tall green corn stalks and fields of soybeans, as far as the eye can see. Little country churches and farm houses are sprinkled about this rich harvest; a portrait of America straight from a Norman Rockwell painting. In the spring and summer months, many people grew gardens full of vegetables that they would can for the winter. Men would hunt and fish, not for sport, but for food. Things moved slow there. It sometimes seems as if time stands still in places like this. Nothing much ever changes. Most people living there are God fearing church going folks and secrets are kept close at hand. Any talk of the paranormal during the time I was a child was usually done in whispers and only between trusted friends or relatives. Almost everyone went to church and attended Sunday school and Satan usually got the blame for anything paranormal. Any talk of aliens would have probably been considered blasphemous. People just didn't speak of such things. You would have been laughed at, ridiculed or quite possibly sent to the nearest mental hospital. Even though those kinds of reactions still happen today it was the rule rather than the exception in those days. A real life Mayberry? Well not quite, but it was a simple life and the one I was born into.

I didn't know it at the time, but I had led a sheltered life during those first few years. Crime almost didn't exist there. Neighbors watched out for each other and no one bothered to lock their house unless they were going to be gone for several days. Those were the days when one could let their children play in their yard without constant supervision and not have to worry about their child being kidnapped. I spent most days doing just that. I loved the outdoors and would spend several hours every day playing cowboys and Indians, drawing things in the dirt with a stick or playing with whatever toy was around to amuse and entertain myself. I was only five years old, and my life to that point was nothing out of the ordinary. My father had left my mother and me when I was only two years old, but she had later remarried to a wonderful man who treated me well, and for me, life, as I knew it, was good!

Although we were poor, very poor, I never came to that realization. I didn't know anything any different than being poor; what it was like to have more or to be wealthy. We did finally get a small black and white television, around that time, but I never watched it that much. Those were the days before cable and one had to rely on "rabbit ears" or some wires from your TV hooked up to an outside antenna. Unlike most other kids, television never really interested me that much at that age. I don't have any memories of watching it before I was five years old, so television had had no influence on my life at all as does happen with some young children. I had never seen a monster movie, a scary TV show or a frightening cartoon series. I had never heard anyone ever talk about monsters or ghosts or anything in that realm, and I certainly had never heard of aliens. At that time, in the early 1960's, there wasn't the media influx of images containing aliens.

Sure there had been movies about UFOs and aliens. There had been books, magazines and comics on the subject, but I had never seen any of it. I had never seen a movie at that time of any kind. I lived in a farm house a half a mile away from the nearest neighbor. The closest town was a twenty minute drive and had a population of just under 1000 people. The closest movie theater and Drive-In Movie was a good forty five minute drive from where we lived. Back in those days, my family couldn't afford to go to the movies anyway.

There are those who would dismiss my early childhood experiences as some kind of delusionary childhood fantasy or blame it all on a vivid imagination. So I am prefacing all of this so as to make clear that, at the time of my first abduction experience, I had never been exposed to anything that would have triggered my young mind's imagination to such an extent or that would have left such a strong impression on my psyche. That first event left such a deep emotional scar that even now, over forty years later, I still have nightmares from it. Nightmares of that first fateful night the visitors came and took me. It's a nightmare that has reoccurred over and over, throughout my entire life. There have been many nightmares about my experiences with these alien creatures, and I have many conscious memories, but it's always been the one about that first night I saw them that will have me screaming out in fear and utter panic in my sleep, until finally waking up with my heart pounding out of my chest as I savor the sweet feeling of relief while coming to the realization that this time it's just a dream.

The old two story farm house we lived in at the time of my first abduction experience had only one bedroom downstairs and three more upstairs that were only accessed by a narrow staircase in the middle of the house which had a door at the bottom of the staircase that when closed would close off the entire upstairs section of the house. There was no central heat or air conditioning so at times during the winter months my parents would close off the upstairs bedrooms to help keep the house warm. They slept in the downstairs bedroom while they would put us kids in the living room area. My younger sister would sleep on the couch, and my Mom would make a pallet of quilts on the floor for my little brother and me to sleep on. It wasn't the most comfortable bed, but at least it was warm. It was early fall, so the nights had started to get chilly. The leaves were starting to change from green to all the golden browns and reds of fall foliage. My parents had moved us into the living room to sleep and had shut off the upstairs for the coming winter months. The night began like any other night. There were no signs to indicate what was about to happen. I crawled under the warm blankets that fateful night, not knowing that my life was about to be changed forever. Innocence was soon to be lost. A life long journey was about to begin that would hide a secret so indelible that it would be many years for any of it to reveal itself.

Sometime during the night, I was awakened by a very bright light from outside the side window of the living room. I raised my head from my pillow and looked in the direction of the light

3

trying to see what it was, but it was to no avail, the light was too bright to see anything. The house was quiet and still. I saw nothing unusual inside the house. My brother was sleeping soundly beside me. My sister was peacefully sleeping on the couch. I don't remember being afraid , but I do remember a strong sense of curiosity came over me.

I thought I heard some sounds coming from the front yard and began to wonder what it was that was making the sounds. We had no outside light, but I could see a glowing light coming through the thin curtain we had over the front window close to our bed and the through the window on the side wall. Something kept calling me inside my head. It felt calming. It wanted me to come to the window to see something. "Don't be afraid, don't be afraid" the voice kept saying, "I have something special to show you." I looked around everywhere for the voice. I knew I could hear it; I just couldn't see where it was coming from. I could stand it no longer. I had to see what it was the voice wanted me to see. I got up from my home made bed on the floor and slowly started to take the few steps toward the front window. The hardwood floor felt cold on my bare feet as I approached the window. I began to feel the brisk cool air in our house, even so, I didn't want to return to the safety and warmth of my bed. Some unseen force kept pulling me closer and closer to the window. I could hear movement outside the window, and yet at that moment, I wasn't afraid. Whatever was controlling my thoughts had made all my fear subside with its promise of showing me something special. Any fear that I had conquered would soon return.

I arrived at the window and lifted my right hand to the left side of the wispy curtains. I didn't hesitate. I pulled open the curtain and saw what will forever be etched into my consciousness. Standing on the other side of the window, within a foot of me, was this creature with a large head; it was looking straight at me with its large almond shaped, deep black eyes. It looked like a giant insect. I wanted to scream. I tried to scream, but it was in vain. Nothing would come out. I was frozen with fear. I took my eyes off of the creature when I saw movement in our yard. We had a big oak tree in the front yard about 15 or so feet away from the window I was looking out of. That was the only tree in the front yard and a field was on the other side of our yard, so it was quite easy to get a good view of the entire front area of the house. As I looked toward the area of the movement, I saw three other creatures that looked exactly like the one by the window. They were small, not much bigger than I was at the time, and very skinny. They were wearing dark colored tight fitting clothing. None of the aliens showed any kind of emotion. They all had the same blank sort of stare on their face. Two of them were standing close to the tree, and the other one was about half way between the creature in front of me and the tree. That one had started to move towards me. I didn't want to, but something forced me to look at the creature in front of me again. I looked into those eyes, eyes that seemed to me like looking into space without any stars. It was like looking into a vast emptiness, devoid of a heart or soul. To this day, I still do not want to look directly into their eyes. This time when I looked into the creatures eyes, I blacked out.

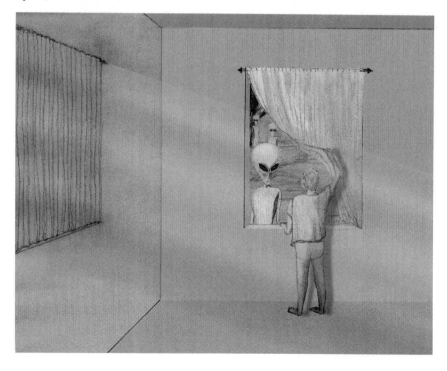

Sketch of the first encounter
©2013 Jeffrey Oldham

When I opened my eyes again, I was on a hard silver colored table. I had gone to bed with underwear and a t-shirt on but I was no longer wearing them. I was lying there completely naked. At first all I could see was a very large bright light that was up over me but more down towards the lower part of my body. I was surrounded by the aliens except at the time I had no idea who or what they were. There were four or five of them around me on both sides of the table. I lay still as I must have been in some kind of shock. I was in utter confusion as to what was happening.

I lifted my head and could see a few more of the creatures in the back of the room. They appeared to be busy doing something. There was a wall of lights and electronic equipment on the right side of me. I started to call out for my Mom, and the aliens took immediate notice. One of them came up, by the right side of the table, and got close to my head. He looked hideous to me! I started to scream profusely for my Mom. "Mommy, Mommy, help me!" I yelled out at the top of my lungs. "Why wasn't she coming to help me?" I thought. "Where was she?" I wondered. I needed her. I needed help! But there was no one to help me. Suddenly, as the one next to me got closer, all the aliens turned into doctors. At least, in my mind they did. I didn't know it then, but in later years I would understand how they use these mind control techniques. They had made me see them as doctors. They reached into my consciousness and pulled out an image of someone I would be familiar with. Someone I would recognize so that I would quiet down perhaps. Now I saw them all wearing the typical doctor's white smocks and they looked human to me. It was all too much for a young boy's fragile psyche; I screamed ever louder. At this point in time, the alien beside me, on the right side, leaned over and raised his hand up to my head. That's the last thing I remember. Everything went black again.

The next day, I had no memory of the events of the previous night. Everything that had happened to me had been suppressed in my memory by these alien creatures that I would in later years come to know as the Greys. I hadn't noticed any physical marks left on my body from the experience, but I was only five years old, and not many five year olds would be looking for any physical signs from the experience left on their body in the first place. I remembered nothing at that time, so I had no reason to suspect anything. No one had said anything about seeing or hearing anything unusual during the night. In my mind, I hadn't yet realized what had happened, or how I would be forever changed by that fateful tragic event. Life resumed back to normal for me. I was still the same happy go lucky little boy I had always been. At least, I was for a while.

Then the nightmares started. I would have these dreams of walking over to the window, pulling the curtain back and seeing the alien staring at me with its big black eyes. I would see the others in the yard. My experience from that night would replay itself over and over in my dreams. I would have the same nightmare of that event, exactly as it happened, and relive the horror again and again, caught in a continual time loop. I would wake up screaming and suddenly jerk myself to a sitting position. The horrific nightmares I kept having seemed too real. "Who are these monsters that are coming after me?" I thought. Their images were now solidly burned into my memory. There was no escape. I remember feeling so confused; I didn't understand what was happening to me. I would tell my mom about the scary little men with their big black eyes. "It's just a dream," she would say. "There are no monsters here. No one is going to take you away," she would tell me as she tried to reassure me, having no understanding or knowledge of what had really happened to me. Neither of us could have ever imagined that this experience was just the beginning of what would be for me, a life time of interaction with these strange looking alien creatures. I would find some comfort in my mother's reassurance when these nightmares would happen, and I would try my best to go back to sleep, but it became increasingly difficult to do so. I didn't want the dream to return so I would fight sleep for as long as I could. I no longer felt safe.

Even now, decades later, I will still occasionally have the same nightmare of that first encounter with the Greys. On numerous occasions, my wife has heard me moaning loudly in fear as if I'm about to scream or sometimes actually screaming out. We have an agreement for her to wake me as soon as she hears me doing this. She has said that sometimes it has been difficult to do so. It's as if I'm in so much fear, and so deep into the experience that I can't break free of the nightmare. I am always so thankful to her for waking me and releasing me from reliving that Hell yet again. As you will learn from this book, I've had many alien abduction experiences. Many of those were very unpleasant experiences, yet the very first one is the one that has caused me the most nightmares. It's not that it was the worst thing they, the Greys, ever did to me. I believe it was because of the age I was when it happened that caused that memory to take up permanent residence in my subconscious. It's important for people to understand just how profound the emotional and psychological damage is when these alien abduction experiences happen, and more importantly to understand how much more significant that damage is when these experiences start at such a young age. The fear from that first abduction at such a tender young age was so intense that it has been impossible to get over. Sure, I've felt fear again over the years during these abduction experiences. My emotions have run the gamut, but as time has passed and I came to understand and accept my fate, the fear has subsided. In fact, there have been times that my abductors have been startled by my actions and stepped back away from me. I'll go into greater detail about that later. I eventually learned to harness the fear I felt from the Greys. I've learned to fear nothing and I suppose I can thank them for that, but it took many years before I reached that point.

Later that winter my family had all gathered around our small black and white TV to watch a movie. It was very cold in our house, so we all covered ourselves with blankets as we settled in to watch the movie. I remember being so excited about it because my Mom had told us kids that it was a very special movie that all kids loved. The movie was "The Wizard of Oz." It was the first movie I ever watched. I was mesmerized right away. My eyes were glued to the screen as the tornado hit and Dorothy's house went flying through the air. I remember feeling so worried about her and her little dog. When Dorothy landed in Oz, it was magical to me; all the wonderful, colorful characters and music. I absolutely loved it! My Mom had been right. This movie was special. I was laughing and feeling very happy as I watched Dorothy, The Tin Man, The Cowardly Lion, The Scarecrow and Toto on their trek to Oz. I couldn't decide which character I liked best. I loved them all. I was enjoying my first movie immensely until the part came on with the flying monkeys. The wicked witch with her scary snarl and screechy voice didn't bother me. It was those flying monkeys that I couldn't take my eyes off. I began to feel very afraid. "I don't want to watch it anymore," I told my Mom and Step Dad. That was met with a stern "be quiet and watch the movie" response from my Mom. So I tried to continue watching. As the monkeys flew out of the castle, I got more and more scared. When they grabbed Dorothy it was too much for me. I began to scream hysterically. This was not my nature as a kid to cry or be upset. I wasn't one to frighten easily, so this was completely out of character for me to react in such a way.

At this point, my Mom realized that something unusual was going on with me. She was able to calm me down and told me that I could hide my head under the covers and hold my hands over my ears anytime the flying monkeys were on the screen. I took her advice and would quickly shield myself from those parts of the movie when they came on. It took years for me to understand that the images of those flying monkeys had triggered my repressed memories of the Greys. They were small and skinny with big eyes. They were intelligent, and they flew through the sky. They were bad, and most importantly, they took people against their will. This combination of images and events had once again awakened what lay hidden deep within me.

Several months went by without any nightmares. I hadn't thought about the hideous creatures in my dreams for quite a while. Everything was beginning to go back to normal. Summer was here and my parents had once again opened up the entire house. I was now sleeping upstairs and sharing a bedroom with my younger brother. The weather was starting to get hot outside. At night, my Step Dad would open the upstairs windows to cool off the house so we could sleep more comfortably. It was on one of those balmy summer nights that the visitors came again.

Sometime during the night I was awakened by a very bright light coming from outside the bedroom windows. The light filled up the bedroom. "Was it morning already?" I asked myself. I couldn't figure out why no one else in the house was awake but me. I thought that maybe I had just awakened before everyone else. I got out of bed and went to the window to look outside. The light was so bright I couldn't see much of anything. I decided to go downstairs to see if my parents were up. I walked out of the bedroom and as I approached the narrow wooded stairwell I heard an unfamiliar voice say my name. "Who's calling my name?" I wondered. "We must have company", I thought. I made my way to the bottom of the stairs which led to the kitchen on the left side and to my parent's bedroom on the right side. I looked into my parent's bedroom and saw that they were sound asleep. I didn't want to disturb them, so I thought I would just go see who was calling me.

Our house had a mudroom beside the kitchen with an entryway that everyone used most all the time. This is where I thought the voice was coming from. This was the door everyone used to enter our house, so it made sense that whoever was here would be calling me from that door. The mudroom had a series of small windows along one outside wall. These windows faced an open field and a large barn on the left side. As I opened the door from the kitchen to the mudroom, I noticed that the bright light had disappeared, and it was now dark again. I didn't have much time to dwell on my confusion as to what was happening. I took just a few steps into the mudroom when two of the Grey aliens popped up in the side windows. I stopped and stood motionless staring at them. It felt like time stood still. I don't know if I was simply frozen in fear and couldn't muster the courage to cry out for help or if they were controlling me and preventing me from doing so. I was helpless. I couldn't move. I tried to scream, but nothing came out. Nor could I speak. All I could do was stand there and stare into the faces of these monsters. The small thin alien spoke again as he stared at me with those lifeless eyes. "We're not here to hurt you. We are your friends," he said as he attempted to persuade me into believing him. "We want you to come with us for a little while," he continued. I felt compelled to obey him. I was able to move again and began to walk towards the mudroom door. I opened the door and walked out onto the concrete porch. The creatures walked around the side of the porch and up to the edge where I was standing.

I was only a child, but I felt like a giant as I looked down upon them from the height of the back porch. They walked over to the steps and reached up for me. I couldn't resist. I was so far under their control I didn't even try to resist. I willingly held out my hand as the alien on the left side raised his arm to get a hold of me. As I stepped down, the other alien came along my right side and wrapped his long spindly fingers around the upper part of my arm. Another Grey was beside him, walking close by. We began to walk slowly away from the house and toward the field. We hadn't walked very far when I felt myself feeling very light, almost a weightless feeling, and then I blacked out.

The next thing I remember is being awake and sitting on a bench type platform seat that was cushioned on the seat and had no back to it. I was still in my t-shirt and underwear that I had gone to bed in that night. The area where I was sitting seemed to be a section of a much larger room. It was all brightly lit. I don't recall seeing what the light source was. A larger, taller Grey alien creature was sitting beside me, to my right. Standing directly in front of me was what looked like one of the aliens who had taken me. There was another bench type seating area directly behind him with a short wall behind it that two other aliens were standing motionless by. They were all staring at me. I was frightened until the tall one sitting beside me lightly touched me with his left hand at the bottom of my neck. He began to communicate with me. I didn't understand how he was speaking with me. I could hear his words and yet I didn't see his mouth move. His words, or, perhaps his touch, had a very calming effect on me. He spoke in what sounded like a very soft monotone voice that I could hear in my head. "We're not going to hurt you" he said. "We are your friends." "Do you understand?" He asked. I nodded my head yes, thinking in my innocent naive way that I wasn't supposed to talk out loud either. He continued, "We want to learn about you." "Can we come and visit you sometimes?" "OK", I muttered. "Oops!" "I'm not supposed to talk out loud" I thought to myself as I slightly raised my head up to look at the reactions of the other creatures. It didn't seem to matter to them. They hadn't moved. They were still just standing there motionless staring at me. He went on to tell me that sometimes when we visit each other that I could play with other children. I asked if they were nice of which he answered that they were. At that time, I felt that the tall one was much nicer than the other ones. I felt more at ease with him than I did with the others. I believed what he was telling me.

He had already begun the process of getting inside my head, and it was working. I knew he was different. Even at the age I was then, I could tell the difference between him and the others. He was larger, he was taller, and he was dressed differently. He seemed to be in control. He took my fear away and acted as if he actually cared about me. I thought he was nice. He communicated to me much as a Grandfather would talk and interact with his Grandson. He had done a masterful job of winning over a young boy's trust. I didn't understand what was happening or why it was happening, but the dye had been cast. A bond was being formed. It was a bond that would be used against and at times for me for many years to follow. I had nothing in this strange place they had taken me to. I had no one. I saw nothing that looked even vaguely familiar. I was afraid and confused by these events. So naturally I grasped onto the only thing there that offered me any degree of comfort and friendship; even if it was some monstrous looking creature. It was all I had. The effect that this tall alien being had on me has lasted my entire life.

Even now, all these years later, I still feel it. After all the things that they've done to me and put me through that has left me at times full of anger and rage, I still feel it. There is a part of me that is unable to let go of the connection I had and have with this tall being that first comforted me on that night so long ago. The control these aliens have over us is really difficult for most people to comprehend, in our limited mental capabilities. Only those who have gone through the same kind of alien abduction experiences could come close to fully understanding how, through all the anguish caused by these alien interactions, I still could feel the strength of this bond.

The next morning, I awoke with no memory of the previous night's experience. No one had heard me walking around the house. No one had heard me opening and closing the door to the mudroom. To this day, I have no memory as to how long I was gone that night or how I was returned. Once again, these alien visitors had buried these memories deep into my subconscious where they would remain for many years, waiting to reveal themselves and the truths they held. They had done what they came to do. They had accomplished their mission and found what they were looking for. How pleased they must have been to find new stock to use. They didn't care about the psychological or physical effects of what they had done to me would and did have. They cared only about their own agenda.

I now believe that I was chosen because someone else in my family had also been an abductee. I have no way of knowing for sure if that is indeed the case. No one in my family has ever talked about anything pertaining to it except my Mother who had told me one time that she had a dream that seemed very real. When she was around 13 or 14 years old, she dreamed that she was inside of some kind of aircraft that had a lot of sophisticated equipment in it much like what she imagined the cockpit of a jet would have. She had never been in an airplane, at that time, so it was a curious dream. She recalled that, in her dream, there were strange looking men there who put her in some kind of chair that leaned back. She also remembered that these men were doing stuff to her. She didn't elaborate, and I didn't press her to. Nothing else has ever been said of it since. It's something she won't discuss. I've often wondered if she too had had these alien abduction experiences. Maybe it was just too much for her to handle, so it has remained locked away in her subconscious forever.

I believe the Greys are looking for a particular DNA. Perhaps they prefer the Native American/Celtic mix that I am. When they find the DNA mix in a family they want, they will not only stay with that family and use various members of the family that meet the criteria they are looking for, but they will test the young of that family at an early age to find out if their DNA hasn't been altered and is still the one they want. They know what works for them. They know, for whatever reason, the DNA code that best serves their purpose. I believe that is the reason why they took me when I was so young. I was chosen because they knew they had a very good chance of finding the DNA they could use at a later time when they began to take sperm from me. They choose me, tested me and tagged me. There would be no escaping them. My fate had been sealed. The creatures waiting for me behind the curtain had made sure of that.

# Chapter 2.

# Signs

Those early experiences I had with these small thin insect looking beings were just a precursor of what would become a lifelong history of events that would affect me in ways I could not have imagined. The signs of the trauma induced by these creatures slowly began to surface, and yet, no one recognized any of them. I can't blame my parents or any of my family for not noticing these odd physical or behavioral traits that I began to develop. I'm sure they must have thought that some it was a bit odd but nothing serious enough to warrant looking into it any further. After all, they had no way of knowing the truth. I'm not sure any of them could have fully comprehended the magnitude of what had happened to me. It was against everything they believed in. Would they have even accepted or believed it had I remembered it at the time and told them? I sincerely doubt it. They would have simply passed it off as my imagination or wild fantasy. No one would have asked me any questions and wanted any details. I'm sure there are some members of my family who to this day will still not be able to accept it, just as there are millions of other people on this planet would still continue to believe that we are alone in the universe. But as time went on the signs were everywhere and very obvious. Still, no one took notice.

Later that same summer, after having the second abduction experience, I had traveled to Mount Vernon with my Mom. I don't recall my brother and sister being along with us on this trip. Mount Vernon was and still is the largest city in the area close to where I lived. It was quite an event to go into the "city" as we called it. It was a warm day. The sun was shining bright in a clear blue sky. It was a great day for a trip to the city, but I didn't feel excited. I sat silently and stared out the window looking out at the farm fields and sporadic patches of trees and woods that quickly passed from my sight as our car sped along the highway. I had started to become forlorn and quiet about that time. I had begun to withdraw and became very shy. It was beginning to show. As we entered the city, my mother explained to me that she needed to stop at the bank. When we approached the bank, she found a parking space on the street very close to the front door. The bank sat on the corner of an intersection. The front door was placed in the corner to where it split both streets but faced neither. My Mother parked the car and came around to my side of the car. I was sitting in the back seat. She took hold of my hand as I got out of the car. "Stay close to me and behave yourself," she said in a firm tone as we walked inside the bank. I stood quietly beside her as we patiently waited our turn in line. I had never been in a bank before. I was enjoying myself as I looked with a deep interest at my surroundings. I was amused by all the people dressed so nice and all the fancy furniture. I never said a word the entire time we were in the bank.

My Mother finished her business and once again took my hand as we left. When we walked out the front door, I looked up to see a large black man standing on the corner of the street waiting to cross. I froze in fear! I had never seen a black person before. He must have noticed me staring at him with this scared look on my face because he smiled and said hello to me. I'm sure it was his kind way to ease my fear of him. It didn't work. When he spoke I went into hysterics. Something about seeing someone who looked different than me had triggered something in my brain. I can only assume that this harsh reaction I had stemmed from the abductions by the Greys. I'm sure seeing this man ignited those memories and set off these extreme emotions I was feeling. I screamed "don't let him take me, don't let him take me Mommy"! My Mom rushed me to the car and quickly got me inside. I hunkered down like a scared rabbit. "Let's go Mommy"! "Hurry, hurry"! By this time, the light had changed, and the man had walked across the street and away from us. My Mother was very upset with me as one would expect. "What is wrong with you"? "Why did you act like that?" She asked me as she went on to tell me how much I had embarrassed her. I couldn't answer. I didn't know. I remember that the rest of the time we were in the city I was constantly looking around still worried that the different looking man would come for me. Different looking men would come for me alright. Far different than the nice man I saw that day in front of the bank.

Nothing else unusual happened to me for several months after the incident at the bank. My Mom had told my Step Dad, and a few close relatives about my reaction to the man at the bank and they had all gotten a good laugh from it. I got some good natured teasing from everyone about it too which I didn't feel was very funny nor could I understand why they thought it was so funny. I sank further inside of myself as time passed. I began to develop a fear of the dark. Of course, as all kids are, I had always been a little uncomfortable in a dark room or outside by myself, but those fears had now substantially increased. I never wanted to go into a dark room or be outside at night by myself. I would lay awake at night trying to go to sleep not knowing why I couldn't relax and sleep. I began to dread the night and the thought of having to go to bed. I would tell my Mom that I wasn't sleepy and didn't want to go to bed, but it never worked. I would have to go to bed anyway so I would lay there afraid to close my eyes and yet afraid to keep them open too; afraid of the darkness, of what may be there in that vast black emptiness. The sense of dread upon going to bed at night stayed with me for many years, and to this day there are times I still sometimes feel it. I know that this is their time. The time the visitors come, and there is nothing I can do to stop them.

As I became more and more withdrawn and quiet I started to lose my sense of security that all young children should feel; I didn't live in a high crime area, but I never felt safe. I always had this fear that someone was going to take me away and do bad things to me; that they would take me so far away I would never be able to come back. I started to distrust people. Even some people I knew but especially strangers. The signs were becoming more and more prominent, but unfortunately for me, no one noticed. Eventually, some of my memories of my time with the Greys began to surface ever so slightly. I would tell my Mother about my new "friends" since they had always tried to convince me into believing that they were indeed, my "friends"

I tried several times to talk to her about the "little men" who would come and get me to go play. "How are your little friends today?" She would sometimes ask. "I haven't seen them today," I would answer. She would just smile. No matter what I would tell her about them because she never took any of it seriously. Why would she really? Lots of kids have imaginary friends. I'm sure she thought that my little men friends were just a cute figment of my imagination. She must have gotten quite a chuckle about it back then. I was so young and naive that I never knew she wasn't taking me seriously; although I often wondered why she never asked me more questions about them.

When I was around 8 to 9 years old, I developed a very strong interest in the paranormal and in space. I would check out books at my school library about the subjects pertaining to these particular areas of interest. Back then you could order paperback books from your Weekly Reader magazine. I always got so excited as I would browse through the new books looking for something to order; hoping for a new book about space or anything supernatural or paranormal. I was fascinated by these subjects and would spend hours with my head buried in one of these books, soaking in the knowledge it had to offer. I suppose this intense interest in this type of material had to be my subconscious mind searching for answers about what had been and still was happening to me. By then I had learned about space, and I had learned about aliens. I had read many stories of people seeing "flying saucers" or disk shaped spaceships, which at that time was the most reported craft. I read the story of Kenneth Arnold and learned of his widely publicized U.S. sighting in June of 1947 when he witnessed nine shiny silver objects flying below him while he was piloting a small aircraft near Mt. Ranier in the Cascade Mountains of Washington state. In one of his reports of the incident, Arnold told a newspaper that the objects moved "like a saucer would if you skipped it across the water." Although Arnold was describing the flight of these objects through the atmosphere and not the shape of the objects, the newspaper report that went out on the AP wire used the term "flying saucer" and thus the term was born.

I remember reading about the now world famous and perhaps best known UFO case ever, the Roswell, New Mexico crash that happened in July of 1947. Of course, at the present time this UFO crash has been written about countless times and featured in many movies and television shows. Back then there wasn't as much known about it as today. I was too young to remember if anyone really believed it happened or not but I don't recall anyone I know ever talking about it. However, I was very interested in the story. When I read the accounts of the aliens they found at the crash site it didn't trigger any of my repressed memories but when I saw drawings of what the crash site was supposed to look like I remember just staring at the eyes of the alien in the drawing. I was drawn to them just as I had been in real life and yet I still didn't understand why.

When I learned of the 1961 alien abduction of Betty and Barney Hill, I felt an odd sense of being familiar with what happened to them. Their reaction and the unparalleled fear that they described, the medical procedures, the communication between them and the aliens and their descriptions of the aliens was all compelling to me but at the same time felt natural. It was like somehow I knew that these things were happening to people, and I knew what was happening during their abduction experiences. I didn't know why I knew these things, but I felt strongly about it. Yet, through it all, the alien mind control that the Greys had done on me held strong. My memories of my own abductions remained locked deep inside my own mind. Still, the signs kept coming.

A couple of years later, I began to open up about my unusual interest. I started to talk to some of my relatives about aliens and UFO's, a subject that had never been mentioned by anyone in my family. I'm sure my inquisitive manner and the questions I asked about these things caught them by surprise. Most of them would simply laugh and tell me that there was no such thing as aliens or they would offer all these various explanations as to what people were really seeing and reporting. Everything from car headlights, airplane and helicopter lights, meteors, or even saying that some people were delusional. That's one that I still hear to this day! None of these explanations satisfied my curiosity and so my quest to learn more continued.

It was during this period of my life that I remember starting to experience paranormal events. Many alien abduction researchers have concluded that there is an abnormal increase in paranormal activity around those individuals that are abductees. I would agree with their hypothesis. This is not a book about ghosts, but I also believe that there is a strong correlation between the increase in paranormal events and abductees. I'm living proof. It is my belief that I have gone through some sort of inter-dimensional shift when I have been taken by the Greys and because of that it has caused the energy or Chi of my body to either increase or vibrate at a much higher level, or possibly both, than most other people. This increase in energy is like a light beacon to spirits/ghosts. They are attracted to me because of it, and they use it for their needs, be it communication, manifestation, touch or to move objects to make their presence known. I am also clairaudient, which is the ability to hear sounds and voices that are outside of the normal range of hearing and not audible to common people. Simply put, I can often hear spirits speaking when others cannot. I have many examples of this phenomenon being verified on digital recordings when played back through audio editing software. I am also able to use this increased level of soul energy to heal. I discovered this ability at an early age too. I attribute all of this to whatever caused my body energy to escalate from these abductions. It is feasible to consider that the Greys are responsible for bestowing this gift upon me. They have done a very good job of watching over my health and well-being all these years. I will talk more about that later in this book.

Once the paranormal events started it was like a floodgate from another dimension had been opened. One of my first ghost sightings actually happened in the daylight. Most people associate ghosts with the dark, but they are just as present in the light but not as easy to see. I was 9 years old at the time and my family had moved once again.

This time we moved to Fairfield, a larger town in southern Illinois. We were in the city, albeit a small one, and lived in a small house, in a typical neighborhood. Next to our house was a large white house that was very old. It hadn't been lived in for many years. I once walked up on the front porch and peeked into the windows. There was still furniture in the house, but it was all covered with large white sheets. Everything was dark and dusty. You could tell that no one had been through that front door in a very long time. Other than peeking through the windows that one time I had never really paid much attention to the old house.

On one particular hot summer day, I was out in my front yard playing with some kids from the neighborhood. I got thirsty and needed water, so I ran inside my house to get a drink. I grabbed a glass and walked to the sink to pour me a glass of water. I gulped the water down quickly as kids will do. As I was setting my glass down, I thought I might as well go to the bathroom while I was in the house so I wouldn't have to interrupt my play time with my friends. The bathroom in that the house was small. One sink, a stool and a bathtub. The bathtub sat up against a wall and under a small window that had individual frosted panes that opened by rolling them out. Because we had no air conditioning, and it was so hot out that day, we had most of the windows in the house open, including the bathroom window which faced the old house next door. I was standing at the stool relieving myself. As I was finishing, I happened to gaze out the bathroom window and look over at the old abandoned house next door. When I looked up to the very top where there was an attic window I was extremely startled! Sitting in the attic window was an old lady staring down at me. She was wearing a black dress that fit tight around her neck with a grey shawl wrapped around her. She had grey hair that was pulled back in a tight bun hair style. She didn't move or make any expression, but I could tell she was looking right at me. I stood motionless for a few seconds while I was looking back at her. Then right before my eyes, she vanished; as if she was never there! I yelled out in terror and ran out of the bathroom. I called for my Mom to come look at the lady in the house. My Mom assured me that there was no one there. She even took me outside, and we looked up at the attic window again and saw no one. But I knew what I had seen. She looked as real as any living person. I never saw her again even though I looked for the ghost of the old lady many times after that. She was the first ghost who revealed to me their reality. She wouldn't be the last.

And so, my venture into the world of the paranormal had now begun. The sighting of the ghostly apparition had further fueled my thirst for knowledge of the unknown. With my abduction experiences firmly planted in my subconscious and now this new realization of the afterlife my journey continued. Everything was quiet for several months until the following spring. My family had again relocated just a short drive away from Fairfield to a very small community called Sims. There was no high school there, and the elementary school consisted of only four rooms in a brick building. There were two grades to each room. I was in 5th grade at the time. On this particular day, all the kids were outside for recess.

It was a bright warm sunny day with beautiful blue skies as far as the eye could see. I was having fun playing with my friends when a kid came up to me and interrupted us. He pulled me aside and pointed to a large black car pulled to the side of the street behind the school. I don't recall if the car was a Cadillac or a Lincoln, but it was one of those and very nice. The kid said, "Those men in that car asked me to come and get you." "What for?" I asked. "I don't know. They didn't say. They just asked me if I knew you and I said yes. Then they asked me to come and get you because they want to talk to you," he replied.

I was always taught to never talk to strangers, but my curiosity got the best of me, so I began walking over toward the fancy car. As I approached the car, I could see two men inside. Both of them were in the front seat. They were dressed in very nice matching black suits and wearing fedora hats. When I got about twenty feet from the car, I hesitated. "Hi Bret," the man on the passenger side who was closest to me said. "Come on over. We're not going to hurt you." He continued, "Your Grandmother is sick and she asked us to pick you up and bring you to her." "Which one," I asked? He didn't give a name and simply said "your mother's mother." I walked to within about ten feet of the car to get a better look at the men. They seemed very strange in both their look and mannerisms and certainly didn't look or act like anyone from around the area I lived in. They were very clean shaven and pale looking. He spoke in a monotone sort of way. I suppose they must not have known this, but I had no relationship with my Grandmother on my Mom's side. I had only seen her a couple of times in my life. I knew that she wouldn't be asking anyone to come pick me up for any reason. I really didn't know the woman. They must have sensed my apprehension as they tried to coax me more. "Come on. Get in" he exclaimed! I could hear the urgency in his voice, and I started to get scared. "You don't know my Grandma, and I'm not getting in the car with you!" I cried out. I turned around toward the school and started yelling for help. As I did, I looked back and saw the car speeding away.

Other kids on the playground had taken notice of my visit from the strange men in the fancy big black car. They had all stood farther back than me, and a couple of them had already gone to alert a teacher who was monitoring recess as to what was happening. The teacher had been up around the other side of the building, toward the front, during my conversation with the two men until he was told of the incident by the other students. I saw the teacher walking at a very fast pace towards me as I was running away from the men in the car. He got a quick glimpse of the car the men were in before it disappeared out of sight but not a good enough look at them to identify either the car or the men. I recounted what had taken place to the teacher and was taken inside to talk to the principal. I repeated the course of events to the principal, and that was it. There was really nothing anyone could do. The closest police were in the next town about 15 or 20 minutes away. The men were long gone by then anyway. No one at the school or in my family could ever figure out who the mysterious men were or why they so adamantly insisted I go with them. It was alarming and I kept a close watch out for them to return, but they never did. At least if they ever did, I don't remember it.

Were these odd men the infamous "Men In Black"? Were they there for me because of my abductions? How did they know my name? Where were they going to take me and what were they going to do with me? As the days turned into weeks, the weeks into months and the months into years, the answers I sought faded further and further away; answers that I will probably never find.

Strange experiences had started to happen to me on a frequent basis, and as they did my interest in the paranormal also became more intense. I constantly searched for answers to the unexplained, the supernatural, the mysteries of our world and the unseen world as well as the worlds I would imagine as I gazed into the heavens. I knew that there was life up there. I was compelled to learn about what and who was among those millions of stars and planets. I had learned to be very selective as to what I asked people with regard to other life forms or even ghosts for that matter. I had learned that the mere mention of aliens would sometimes upset people as it didn't coincide with their religious beliefs. Many times I got Bible quotes said back to me after asking a question or talking about any paranormal, alien or UFO subjects. Sometimes I would get made fun of and laughed at by my classmates or other kids at church when I said anything about these subjects. It was difficult to find anyone with the same thirst for knowledge that I had. I eventually started keeping things to myself. I began not trust anyone enough to speak with them about it without fear of being chastised for my beliefs or interest in these subjects. Even my parents dismissed most of what I would tell them. I was alone, and I was becoming fully aware that I would be alone with these experiences for a very long time. Looking back on it all now, I believe that it made me stronger. I relied on no one to help me through it so I had to learn to deal with it on my own or it would destroy me. I learned to face my fears at a very young age. I became strong to survive, and I survived because I became strong.

When I was in 6th grade, we had moved to New Concord, a small college town in central Ohio. It was there that the nose bleeds started. It was there that the paranormal activity increased dramatically, and it was also in New Concord that I remember getting the nasal implants during an abduction experience.

I have no recollection of getting onboard the craft. My first memory is of opening my eyes and seeing a very bright light directly over my head. I was lying on a silver table with smooth round edges. The light above was so bright that I couldn't see any more of the room I was in or how many of the aliens were there. It was the Greys again, and this time there was one on each side of me and one up by my head. I was unable to move at all. The only thing I could move was my eyes. I tried to open my mouth to speak and couldn't. I felt completely paralyzed. The creature standing by my head put his hand on the top of my head. His long spindly fingers stretched down over my forehead. He was able to tilt my head back slightly. As he did, the Grey on my left side picked up a long thin instrument of some kind that seemed to be glowing or lit in some way. He started to stick it in my left nostril. I closed my eyes but, not because of the device they were sticking in my nose. It was because he was close to me as he was inserting it and I didn't want to look at his eyes. It was quickly over. I don't remember feeling any pain. This time none of the aliens communicated with me. It was all very matter of fact, devoid of any connection with me at all. It was very regimented and seemed as if they were merely doing their job. A routine they had performed many times before it seemed. I never saw the tall one either; just the three small ones who did the procedure on me.

The next morning, I woke up with small blood stains on my pillowcase. At the time, I had some memories of the event from the night before, but after thinking about it, I decided not to tell anyone and dismissed it as a vivid nightmare. I just figured that my nose had started bleeding a little during the night for some unknown reason and didn't really think that much more about it. Within days, I started having frequent nose bleeds. It was very embarrassing at the time. I would get a nose bleed during class at school or while riding on the school bus home. Then, one day, during recess, while I was playing basketball, I got a rather severe nose bleed which was very difficult to stop. The school nurse called my Mom to come and pick me up from school. Enough was enough. She decided to take me to the doctor to get to the bottom of it. I'm sure she was just as concerned as I was as to what was wrong with me. The doctor examined me, and they took blood samples. He gave me some helpful hints on how to stop my nose bleeds when they happened. He couldn't find any reason for the nose bleeds and sent me home. My blood work came back fine also. The doctor couldn't give me a reason as to what was causing these reoccurring nose bleeds. Over the next few weeks, they would happen less and less frequently until they finally subsided. This was only temporary though as I would suffer on and off for years with these unexplainable nose bleeds. I believe that they were the results of having the implant placed into my nasal cavity. There would be several more times over the forthcoming years that I would wake up with blood on my pillow case. It was another sign that no one understood or realized as to what the real cause was.

As the physical signs of my abduction experiences began to surface the paranormal activity around me did so too. My senses began to sharpen. My awareness of these other worldly entities increased. It was around this time that I learned that I was able to hear the spirits speaking. Being clairaudient is something that I've now grown used to. I have many documented cases of being with other people on ghost investigations and telling them that I heard a spirit speaking to me where I've had a recorder also picking up these ghostly voices and verifying what I said I heard.

When I was younger, these abilities would scare me as I didn't fully comprehend what was happening or why it was happening to me. Many times, I would be alone, and hear one of them speak to me. I never told anyone of this. Most of the time I would run or walk away very quickly to get away from the voice. Our house in New Concord had ghosts. They were attracted to me and were constantly attempting to get my attention. They would speak to me when I was alone. Just a word or two but enough to let me know they were there with me. One night I was getting ready to go to bed. I went to the bathroom to brush my teeth. I picked up my tooth brush and spread the toothpaste over the bristles. I was about to reach for the faucet to turn on the water when I saw the water faucet handle slowly begin to turn by itself. The water came shooting out. I was quite startled as you might imagine. I dropped my toothbrush in the sink and turned around to my right toward the bathroom door to leave. I was going to go tell my parents what had just happened. The linen closet was in the bathroom of this house. It was on my right side as I was facing the door. I hadn't gotten the chance to take a single step when I saw the linen closet door handle turning by itself and then the linen closet door swung open. It was too much for a boy my age to witness! I ran out of the bathroom in a panic. My parents were watching a movie in the living room. "The water just turned on by itself in the bathroom!" I exclaimed. I continued," The linen closet door opened by itself!" I was shook up, but they just started laughing at me and told me to go to bed. "I saw it. I saw it," I repeated. They merely shook their heads and kept on watching their movie. "Please, please, you've got to believe me," I pleaded. But my pleas fell on deaf ears. I was told once again to go to bed which I did without ever brushing my teeth that night. It was a long time before I ever felt comfortable in that bathroom.

Unfortunately, for me that wasn't the end of it. The nightly visitations from our ghostly inhabitants started soon after. They wouldn't leave me alone. I shared a bedroom with my younger brother. It was a large bedroom with hardwood floors. We each had a twin bed pushed up against opposite walls. Many nights I would be awakened by someone shaking my bed. I would open my eyes and look around the room. There was never anyone there. As soon as I would start to fall back asleep they would ever so slightly shake my bed again. Sometimes I could hear footsteps walking at a slow pace across the wooden floor.

One cold winter night I was bundled under a pile of blankets in my bed. The house was still and eerily quiet, so quiet that you could almost hear yourself breathing. The air was crisp and a chill filled the house. I had just climbed into bed and had gotten comfortable under the warm pile of blankets. I was lying on my left side facing the wall. I was just about to doze off when I heard the sounds of footsteps in my bedroom. I didn't look up this time. It was too cold, and I was too comfortable. I figured it was my Mom coming in to get something. The footsteps had started over by the bedroom door. I could hear the slow but steady walk coming my way. Clop, clop, clop, clop, until finally the footsteps stopped right beside my bed. I still believed it was my Mother, so I never spoke or turned over to look. I returned to my slumber, but as I did I felt someone getting into bed with me. I could feel the weight as they lay down beside me on top of the blankets. I started to get scared. I lay motionless and pretended to be asleep. The body was right up next to me.

Then I felt someone get very close to my face but not touching me. I wanted to open my eyes, but I didn't have the courage. All of a sudden, I could feel a heavy breath blowing on the upper back side of my head right above my ear. The breathing was so heavy and forced that I could feel my hair moving with each exhale; Whoosh! Whoosh; over and over, in a steady pattern. After feeling several of these heavy breaths, I mustered up the courage to speak. "Mom" I softly muttered. There was no reply. Although I really didn't think that my Mom would be getting in bed and lying beside me; it was worth a try to see since the only other explanation was the one I didn't want to accept. I lay perfectly still as I mustered up the courage to speak again. "Mom" I asked. This time louder than the previous one in the hopes that maybe she simply didn't hear me the first time I asked. The silence I heard next was deafening. Chills ran down my spine. I wasn't brave enough to roll over and face whatever or whomever it was lying beside me. I did what most every kid would do under the unfortunate circumstances I found myself in. I quickly covered my head with blankets and moved over as close to the wall as I could get. I began to pray, "Please God, please make them go away." I repeated the short prayer over and over. It must have worked. I felt the presence move off of my bed. The entity then shook my bed a few times, but I held steadfast in my prayers with my head under the covers. Then finally it was over. I listened intently for any sound in my room and heard nothing. I never came out from under the blankets. I fought sleep until it overtook my fear and I dozed off into a restless slumber.

I've often wondered who or what this presence was and what they wanted with me. To this day, I'm still not sure if it was a ghost, an alien or some other worldly entity. I didn't tell anyone what happened to me. I didn't want to scare my brothers and sister, and I didn't think my parents would believe me anyway since they had so easily dismissed my earlier experiences, but I knew I had to do something to stop it from coming back.

There was a small college in New Concord called Muskingham College. We lived close to the school. I sometimes would venture on to the campus and look around. One day while walking around the campus I decided to go to the college library to look for any books that might help me to know what to do to rid myself of these ghostly visitors. I found plenty of books on ghosts. It was during this research that I learned to empower myself. I learned how they fed on my fear and used that against me. I learned why I was hearing them, how to speak to them and how to control them. I read about the symbolism and power of amulets. I wanted a protection amulet, but I had no idea where to get one. Fate was in my corner though. Not long after that I was with my Mom at a yard sale and there was a basket of junk sitting there. A real hodgepodge of stuff all piled up in an old laundry basket. I was looking through it when I noticed a necklace chain at the bottom of the basket. When I dug it out I found an amulet attached to it. It was the Circle of Protection amulet I had seen pictures of in one of the books at the college library! I was so excited to find it. I went to the man who was having the yard sale and asked him how much it was. "Now why would you want something like that?" he quipped. "I just think it's cool," I quickly answered back. "Do you know what that is for?" He asked. I answered him honestly. "Yes, I read about it at the library" I replied. We looked at each other for a moment without either of us saying a word.

He must have sensed my need because he cracked a slight smile and said, "You can have it for free". "Really? Thank you, thank you very much," I exclaimed. It wasn't so much the amulet itself. It was what it stood for. It was conviction and a belief in myself that I gained through this simple amulet. It was the catalyst for bigger things. I felt good that day. I felt hope. I no longer felt like I wasn't in control of the ghosts that haunted me. A new sense of empowerment was coming over me. I was developing tools to use. I was gaining knowledge that I would use to this day. It was the beginning of when the ghosts that filled my life would do so on my terms, not theirs.

From that day forward, I confronted the ghosts when they would bother me or attempt to scare me. I hung the Circle of Protection amulet on the end of my bed. I would speak out loud to the ghosts before I would go to bed and demand that they leave me alone. They did for a while, and it felt good. My bed stopped shaking at night while I was sleeping. The footsteps stopped. The ghostly voices I heard subsided. If I would hear one I would tell them that I didn't wish to speak to them, and they would leave. Sometimes I felt badly about it, but I needed peace. Little did I know then that I would never find the elusive peace I sought. The spirits would always come back. The aliens would too.

# Chapter 3

# The Awakening

A blanket of thick white snow had fallen the night before turning the rolling hills of Ohio into a large playground for any kid with a sled, toboggan, inner tube or anything else one could find to slide down those slippery hillsides with. It was bitter cold that day. The kind of cold that feels like it's biting your lungs as you breathe; still that didn't stop my brother Jeff, my cousin Lynn and me from going out in it to ride our sleds. There was a large hill behind where we lived that we chose to go sledding on. We slowly trudged our way to the top and looked down at the untouched, virgin snow. Suddenly our weary legs didn't feel so tired nor did freezing temperatures seem to bother any of us. "This is going to be fun," I thought. I'm sure my brother and cousin both felt the same excitement. After all, we were all adolescent boys ranging in age from 11 to 13, and this was the kind of thrill we sought.

My cousin Lynn went first. As he sped down the hill on his sled, we all soon realized that we were going to be sledding very fast as the conditions warranted it. I went next, and it was quite the ride! I had a difficult time controlling the sled and stopping. After we had all made several runs down the hill and making our way back up, we started to get tired. We decided to go one more round and then go home. We had all experienced a couple of wipeouts without anyone being injured. That was about to change.

At the very bottom of the hill was a concrete utility building. We had all been easily steering away from it and coming to safe stops. My brother Jeff started down the hill on his last run that afternoon.

Lynn and I were waiting for Jeff to take his before taking ours. On his way down, Jeff hit a large bump in the snow which threw him off course. Before he had any time to recover, he plunged head first into an old toilet that was sitting in the back of the utility building. He lay there motionless as Lynn and I ran to him. He had been knocked out by the blow. We rolled him over and saw that he was still breathing. We called his name and patted his cheek to bring him to. After what felt like an eternity but what were probably just a few seconds he came around. We helped him to his feet. He was still groggy and dizzy and was complaining about how bad his head hurt. He had a very large lump come up on the upper right side of his forehead. Lynn and I got on each side of him and helped him walk home.

There was no adult's home that day. It was just us. The lump on the side of my brother's head looked really bad. I had never seen anything like it before. Jeff was coherent but still in a lot of pain. We were all worried about him but didn't know what to do. I got some ice and wrapped it in a washcloth to put on Jeff's head in the hopes that it would help the swelling go down and ease his pain. After a few minutes, we checked the lump, but nothing had changed. I became worried that maybe Jeff had sustained a serious brain injury. At first I began to panic but then a strange sensation filled my body. I became very calm. Something inside me told me to use my energy to help Jeff. "I'm going to put my hand on the lump and use God's light to help you," I told my brother. He agreed to let me try. I don't know why I felt compelled to do it, but I did and as I did I asked God to send his energy through me and to let me use my energy to take away the lump.

I was in a zone. I could feel the energy surging through my body. As it did, I directed it through my arm and out my hand into Jeff's injury. As I continued, I could feel the lump getting smaller. I tried even harder. I told my cousin Lynn, "put your hand on top of mine." Instead, he just put his hand on my wrist and tried his best to help. I took my hand away to look at the lump. "Look at it now," Lynn cried out in amazement! It was amazing. The lump was still there but had greatly reduced in size. It didn't look nearly as bad as it did before. Then Jeff told us that his head felt a lot better. We were all relieved. We talked about what had just happened. "How did you do that?" Lynn asked. I had no answer.

That day was the beginning of my awakening. That was the day that I came to the realization that there was something different about me, and I needed to find out why. It was on that day and because of that single event that my whole mindset began to change. I started to think about things differently. I started to question the religion I had been taught. I started to question all religion. From then on, I no longer accepted something as the truth just because someone said it was. I looked at my life with a new perspective. I no longer cared that I was different. In fact, I embraced it. I was on the road to discovery and not afraid of where it would lead me to. I spent many hours by myself in deep contemplation about my life and all the strange and unusual things that had happened to me. I pondered the reasons I was able to transfer and use the energy as I had done for my brother. "How did I know to do that?" I asked myself time and time again. "How was I able to do that?" I wondered. The answers were out there waiting for me to find them. It would take several more years, but I would get my answers.

During those years of reflection on my life, it occurred to me that I had unusually good health. It was something that I had never really given thought to before. I suppose I simply took it for granted but other than a few sore throats through my childhood I hadn't been sick with anything. I now believe that even those early throat infections stemmed from sinus problems triggered by the implants the Greys had put in me. The older I got the better my health got. From the time I was 11 or 12 years old I had pretty much stopped getting sick with anything. I knew that wasn't the case with most kids or adults either for that matter. It was another oddity that I discovered about myself. It was another question I would add to the list. What is so different about me? Why am I so lucky to never get sick? The list of questions grew longer.

When I was a sophomore in high school something changed from the norm. I got sick; very sick. I suddenly started losing weight and running high fevers. I got weaker by the day. I went to the doctor only to find out that he couldn't figure out exactly what was causing this strange sickness that came upon me. He wasn't even sure which treatment I should follow. I kept losing weight. Five pounds, then it was ten pounds. I got weaker and weaker from the sickness that had overtaken me. The weight kept falling off. Fifteen pounds, sixteen pounds and then finally twenty pounds lost in just a couple of weeks. Nothing the doctor gave me was working. I got so weak that I was unable to make it up the stairs to my bedroom. I started sleeping on the sleeper sofa. I began to black out when I would get up and try to walk. They started talking about hospitalizing me, but my family had neither insurance nor the money to pay an exorbitant hospital bill. I thought I might be dying. The doctors couldn't figure out what was wrong with me. The medicine they gave me didn't appear to be working. I was so weak I couldn't walk without assistance from someone. I had never been so sick before nor have I since.

Then one night I had a dream. At least, I thought at the time it was a dream. I saw aliens in my dream. They told me that I was going to get well very soon. I woke up that morning remembering the strange dream from the previous night. I felt hungry. "That's unusual," I thought to myself. I hadn't had an appetite in days. I asked my Mom to make me some bacon and eggs, which she did, and I proceeded to eat almost all of it. The rest of the day continued the way it started. I was so hungry; I ate again at lunch and then again at dinner. I was able to get up and walk by myself. I was still extremely weak, but I could feel my strength slowly coming back. By the next day, I felt like a new person. Whatever sickness had come over me had left. I kept thinking about the dream of the aliens and how they told me that I was going to get well. "Was there some connection?" I wondered. "Why would I have a dream like that?" I kept asking myself.

A few days later I happened to have my shirt off and was at the kitchen sink getting a drink of water. My Mom came up behind me. She was standing there waiting to use the sink. All of a sudden she says, "Hold still and lean over a bit". "Why? What's wrong?" I asked her. "You have a large red mark on your lower back. It looks like a scar and is really big", she replies. I had no idea what she was talking about. I went into the utility room where we had another sink with a mirror and did my best to see what she was referring to. "What do you think caused this?" I asked her. "I don't know. It looks like you've been cut or something", she said with a puzzled look on her face. "I'll call our doctor about it and see if he wants you to come in", she said. "Ok, but I feel fine now so don't worry about it", I said. My Mom did call our family doctor to tell him about the scar she had found on my back. He told her that scars like that were very common on young boys my age and attributed it to stretch marks without ever having examined me. That was a good enough explanation for both me and my mother and at the time we both readily accepted it as the cause of the scar on my lower back. I would eventually change my mind of how that scar came to be as that scar was not the only one left on my body by my strange visitors over the years. Even then, I couldn't help wondering if it was connected to my alien dream I had before I started getting well. The veil was being slowly lifted. The awakening continued....

Something else dramatically changed in the months following my bizarre illness. I began to get an intense interest in all things metaphysical. For the first time in my life, I had started to question some of the things in the Bible. I opened up to other religions with an open mind and yet remained skeptical of any that claimed to be the real truth. Hinduism, Buddhism, Mormonism; I started reading and learning about them all. I read books from eastern Yogi's such as Paramahansa Yogananda's "Autobiography of a Yogi" and teachings from the famed guru Sai Baba. This was very unusual behavior for someone in my family.

Something had happened to me during the time I was sick that had changed my whole belief system and how and what I perceived as the truth. It was these changes that would eventually help lead me to the events that would unlock what the Greys had thought they had safely hidden away in the dark crevices of my mind.

As I entered further into my teens, I experienced even more changes. I started having bouts with depression. Until I became so ill, I had always been a relatively happy person. After my sickness I would go through these periods of immense darkness and sadness. I didn't know why. These bouts of depression would be a lifelong demon and something that even now I struggle with from time to time. Sometimes I would have anger issues surface. It seemed parts of my personality were changing, and I couldn't merely chalk it up to teenage angst. It went much deeper than that. I was a gifted athlete and playing sports helped considerably to ease my depression and inner anger. I taught myself to play guitar and started writing songs and poetry. It was all a release. An outlet to subdue what was trying so hard to surface in my consciousness. The closer I got to the awakening, the more intense these inner demons became.

I now know why I felt the way I did. I know that those feelings of helplessness produced during those multiple abduction experiences transformed into feelings of anger. To people who have never had to endure an alien abduction experience it may be hard to comprehend what it does to the abductee's psyche. It may be difficult to understand what it is like to be taken against your will and subjected to intense emotional experiments that are nothing more than an illusion created by your captors to monitor your emotional reaction to the scenario, or to understand how it feels to be totally helpless to do anything to stop them. Only an abductee knows that to be an unwilling participant in sexual procedures is akin to being raped over and over. Your life is not your own, and you have no control over that. You have no control over what they decide to do to you. You have no control over when and how many times they will take you. You have no control over any of it. You learn to become strong both mentally and physically, or you succumb and let it ruin your life. I chose to become strong.

During my late teen years, the disembodied voices I had heard since early childhood stopped. I went for several years without hearing them. I went for two or three years without having any sort of paranormal activity at all, and I liked it. I thought that they had finally left me alone, although I wasn't sure why they did, but I really didn't care. I was enjoying true peace and tranquility. For the first time in my life, I felt as close to normal as I ever would. I still maintained my interest in the paranormal. I still read books and magazine articles about ghosts, UFO's and all things mysterious. I just wasn't experiencing anything unusual. My interest in metaphysics grew stronger. I was still reading and studying various religious books and texts yet I would always go back to metaphysics as the thing that made the most sense to me. I've always felt that this all stemmed from what I had learned from the Greys; that they must have influenced my beliefs unbeknownst to me at the time.

Whatever the reason, I was opening my mind up to the broader spectrum of life and all things in it during this time. It set a precedence for a thought process and ways of looking at things that would never leave. I found many truths in the knowledge I was absorbing; truths that I could accept and believe in; truths that I found out for myself and not just believed because someone else told me that it was the truth. It was liberating and yet the real liberation was drawing closer day by day.

By the time I reached my 20's I was well versed in the subject of UFO's and most all things paranormal. I had studied Hinduism, Mormonism, Buddhism, Christianity and Metaphysics. I had studied psychic phenomena and channeling. I even attended several channeling sessions where people claimed to have been channeling some ancient wise being. They all seemed the same to me, and I quickly lost interest in channeling. I started going to as many psychics as I could afford to go to. Once I went to five different psychics in the same day just as an experiment to see if they were all going to tell me the same things since it was all in the same day. They didn't. I learned how the fake psychics manipulate people and fish for answers. I started to be able to use my own instincts to sense and feel the energy of those who had real psychic ability. I searched for mediums. I wanted to meet someone else who could hear the dead as I did when I was younger. When I finally did it was an amazing experience, one in which more truths from my past came to the forefront.

To protect her privacy, I will not use her real name. I will call her Mary. Mary was from South America and had one child, a girl who at that time was 12 years old. Mary had clinically died giving birth to her daughter and was brought back to life. When she recovered she discovered that she had her psychic ability and had used it ever since to help people. She was deeply religious after the NDE (near death experience). Her daughter was an extremely advanced child who had been tested to have a genius IQ and was taking college courses at 12 years of age. Something very special had indeed happened to Mary and to her daughter when she gave birth to her.

I went to Mary for answers just like everyone else does who goes to see a psychic or a medium. I wasn't looking to speak to any relative on the other side. I wanted to know why I heard the spirits speak and I wanted to know what message any of them had for me. Mary greeted me at her door with a warm smile. As she shook my hand, I knew right then that she was genuine. I could feel the positive energy pulsating through her body. She walked me back to her home office where she conducted her readings. When I walked through the office doorway, I immediately saw a painting of Jesus above a small wooden altar to my left. The altar had a couple of small candles on it that were burning. There was a gold metal tray sitting on top of a black velvet cloth which I assumed was an offering tray. Mary never asked me for any money or even discussed with me how much her reading was. I was impressed by this but still needed to know, so I asked her. She simply asked me to offer whatever I felt it was worth but to place it in the tray under the painting of Jesus.

She explained that hers was a gift from God and that she only did readings for people who were spiritual with a strong belief in God. She looked straight at me and said, "I don't have to ask you if you believe." "I already know you are a very spiritual person with very good energy," she continued. "She had picked up on my energy just as I had on hers," I thought to myself. I knew I was in for a special night.

After a brief prayer and meditation, Mary began the session. "You're not afraid of the spirits are you?" She stated. "No, I'm not afraid at all," I replied. I was stunned that she had picked up on that so soon. She then told me that she had contact with her spirit guides and that I could ask my questions. I had made a list of questions and hoped to get to as many of them as possible. I asked question after question and was amazed at the accuracy of her answers. She told me things about myself that there was no way she could know. She explained to me that the spirits were attracted to me because of my energy and for the kind of person I was. I was amazed. At last! I had finally found the real deal; a genuine medium!

Suddenly a strange new fragrance filled the room. It smelled like the scent of fresh flowers. Before I could say anything to Mary about what I smelled she spoke, "there is someone here from the spirit world who wishes to communicate with you." She continued, "I'm trying to get his name." I sat anxiously waiting to learn who this spirit Mary was speaking with might be. Then, without hesitation, she says, "Nelson." I immediately know who she is talking about, but I keep quiet. "He says he is your uncle," she states. "Yes, that's right," I reply. I wondered why my uncle Nelson would be trying to speak with me. "What does my uncle Nelson want to say to me?" I asked. "He has a message for someone that he wants you to deliver for him," Mary answers. I ask who it is. Mary says she is having trouble understanding or hearing the name of the person to whom my uncle Nelson is referring to. Mary keeps asking him to say the name again and explains that she can't get the full name. She says it's a name that sounds like it starts with an "m" but doesn't seem to get any further with it. I'm pretty sure I know what name she is attempting to enunciate, but once again, I don't respond. I don't want to offer any help so as to make sure the information is coming from the other side and not me. "He's rubbing his eyes." "It's the woman with the sore eyes," she tells me. Now she has lost me. I thought I may have known who it was that my uncle Nelson wanted me to deliver his message to but I didn't know anyone with sore eyes or even what it meant for that matter. I shrug my shoulders as I shake my head and tell Mary that this means nothing to me. She then again asked for a name and speaks out loud as she is going through the names. "Marge, Marie, Martha." "Martha!" "Yes, that's it!" She exclaims. Martha was my aunt and Nelson's wife who at that time was still alive. It was very emotional for me. I knew I was speaking with my deceased uncle. Not just hearing a couple of words or maybe a sentence like what I would get but having an actual conversation albeit a limited one.

Mary went on to tell me things that my uncle told her that he and I had done when I was a child. Things like, when we built a wagon together and when I helped him build a small horse barn. These were things that Mary would have had absolutely no way of knowing. My uncle had told Mary to ask me to tell my aunt Martha about him coming through to Mary and would I please let her know that he was okay and happy. He wanted her to let go and stop grieving so much for him. I promised him that I would tell her. It was a promise I kept. I found out later that my aunt Martha was about to have cataract surgery. That was what my uncle Nelson had meant when he was referring to the "sore eyes". This was something that even I didn't know about, let alone Mary.

After the spirit of my uncle left Mary asked if I had any more questions, she answered a couple more but then stopped abruptly. Then she looked at me with an odd look on her face. "You have had some very strange experiences," she softly said. "I see very sophisticated equipment around you with lots of lights and buttons." Her voice became solemn as she softly said, "bad things have been done to you, and you are very angry about it." I was speechless. I had no response as I didn't know what she was talking about at the time. "You have to learn to release the anger and accept the things you can do nothing about or change," she continued. "Ok, I will work on that," I answered back still not knowing what exactly she was talking about.

The session ended soon after that. I thanked Mary and left her $50.00 on the offering tray which was a very fair sum for such an inspirational and emotional reading. On the way home that night I didn't turn on the radio. Somehow the silence seemed appropriate. I was in deep thought. I drove down the busy streets of Las Vegas completely oblivious to the world around me as I ignored the glaring white glow from the headlights of the passing traffic. The large bright street lights flashed on my car as I passed under them in a steady rhythm. I kept thinking about Mary's answers to my questions that she received from the spirits. I thought that I should do something in return to help the spirits. I thought about how I was going to explain to my aunt Martha in order to relay the message from my uncle to her. Mostly though, I thought about the part towards the end when Mary told me about seeing the "sophisticated equipment" around me and about the "bad things" that had been done to me but I had no memory of these "bad things" that Mary was referring to. She had been so accurate on everything else she had told me. How could she have been wrong about these things? It bothered me almost to the point of obsession. Yet still I had no answers.

Music had always been a love of mine. I had taught myself to play guitar and had become a very good guitar player. I played in various bands from my teens and all through my twenties. For a few years in my early twenties, I was playing shows almost every night. At this point in my life I had already played hundreds of shows from small local bars to large concert stages for several thousand people. I started to have dreams that I couldn't understand. I would wake up in terror from some of these nightmares. These dreams involved aliens. I was also suffering from sudden bouts of depression for absolutely no reason. I always simply dismissed it all and tried to find some rational explanation as to the cause for both the dreams and depression. I began to drink heavily and started smoking cigarettes. I was on a quick path to self-destruction and I didn't know why.

One night at a gig, right before taking the stage, I suffered an anxiety attack. It was crippling and like nothing I had ever felt before. I was finally able to calm down enough to do the show with the help of some alcohol, but nothing would ever be the same again.

The panic attacks kept coming. I got to the point that I didn't want to leave the house. The smallest incident would trigger them. Things as mundane as waiting in line at the bank or getting caught in traffic congestion or even attending sporting events where there were large crowds. They were taking over my life, and I knew I had to get help. I couldn't understand why this was happening to me. I had never been afraid of much of anything. I had been in front of crowds for most of my life. I had played several sports throughout my youth and had been a star basketball player winning numerous awards. I had been on stage performing music in front of people for years. Now all of a sudden, I was afraid to leave my house. It was the only place I felt safe. It made no sense to me and yet it was very real and happening.

I went to my MD for my panic attacks. It was suggested by him that I see a therapist. I decided to see a hypnotherapist first before seeing a psychologist or psychiatrist. I didn't want to be put on medication if it was something I could resolve myself without it. I never felt that the first hypnotherapist I went to fully understood what I was experiencing or maybe it was just that he didn't seem concerned as to what the cause was but after a few sessions I quit going. I was still having the panic attacks and began to think that I did indeed need medication in order to control them. I happened to come across an ad of another hypnotherapist who had a background in metaphysics and past life regression therapy. I made an appointment with him just to see what he could do differently than the first therapist. My anxiety attacks were getting so bad by this time that I didn't want to drive by myself anywhere, so I asked my mother if she would take me to the appointment. She agreed to take me. The first session went well. He took the time to talk with me, and I felt he was really attempting to get to the root of the problem. We did some simple mind control relaxation exercises, and that was it for the session. I left there feeling very hopeful that he was going to be able to help me.

I began a series of regular therapy sessions consisting of two or three sessions a week. Each time I was learning more and more how to control my thoughts and conduct self-hypnosis on myself. I learned meditation techniques from him and began to meditate on a daily basis. With each passing week, I had less and less of the anxiety attacks. I was gaining control of my consciousness, and I knew it. It felt good as my awareness increased and I realized the power of my own mind. As I gained my confidence back, I began to circulate back into society. I started taking a meditation class every week where I learned how to delve even deeper into my sub and super conscious mind. The anxiety attacks eventually disappeared as I took control back. I became a much calmer person. My awareness and perception of the world changed. I also began to have vivid flashbacks of my alien encounters. I started to have lucid dreams of my many abduction experiences. I came to the realization that these lifelong alien abductions were the reason for the emotional issues I had experienced and had been the real cause of my anxiety attacks. It had all come to a climax. The mental suppression the Greys had placed upon me had  surfaced. Through my hypnotherapy, self-hypnosis and meditation, I had opened up a floodgate of memories that I'm sure the Greys had assumed would never be unlocked. My life would be forever changed with these new revelations. I had finally awakened......

# Chapter 4

# Mind Games

"Where am I?" I silently thought to myself. I was looking into pitch black darkness. I tried to look around, but I couldn't turn my head to do so. I felt paralyzed. I only could move my eyes. I felt the adrenaline rush through my veins as I anxiously tried to figure out where I was and what was happening to me. Then the thought occurred to me that I was dreaming this; that I was having some kind of waking nightmare. "That is why I can't see anything", I concluded as I frantically tried to rationalize my situation. "All I need to do is wake up, and I will be free of this darkness", I surmised. I focused all my energy and thoughts on waking myself. I concentrated on opening my eyes. I desperately wanted to wake up. I wanted to open my eyes and see the light. After what seemed like an eternity I felt my eyes slowly opening. I could see a very bright light filtering in through my eyelids. I had succeeded in waking myself from what I thought was a nightmare only to find the real horror waiting for me in the waking world.

As my eyes opened I found myself looking directly into the face of a Grey who was leaning over me on my right side, only inches away from my face. Those big eyes like endless pits of black tar staring at me completely devoid of emotion. I felt instant terror! Soon I could see two other Greys come up on my left side. I could feel them touching me with metal objects. I felt no pain, only immense fear. The one closest to me on my right side was communicating to me to calm down. He wasn't physically speaking these words but rather was telepathically sending them to me. "We're not going to hurt you", I would hear in my head. "Let me up, please let me up", I frantically pleaded back to him in my thoughts. I tried to calm myself down. "They will do what they want with me and then they will take me home", I thought to myself. As I grew a bit calmer, I realized that I was now able to move my head. I raised my head up from the table and looked around. "Thank you", I sent back to the Grey. I then saw that I was totally naked; laying on a silver examining table that had rounded smooth edges. The other two Greys that had been poking and prodding me before were now just standing a few feet back from me and watching me look around as was the Grey I had been communicating with. This all seemed to be a part of their work. They wanted to observe me and how I reacted to this environment I found myself in. The room was small. It looked almost as if the walls were slightly curved. Nothing had an edge to it; even where the wall ended was rounded. The light in the room was very bright but oddly enough didn't hurt my eyes as one would expect it to. It seemed to be a different kind of light source than I've ever seen. I wasn't able to ascertain as to what was the light source. From my vantage point, I wasn't able to see much more. I laid my head back down on the table and thought, "Oh God! What now?" The next thing I remember was waking up in my own bed.

There was something different this time. When I woke up, I remembered everything that had happened. It seemed that they were beginning to lose the mind control they had used on me for so many years to suppress my memories of my encounters with them. All the meditation and hypnosis that had opened up all these repressed memories not only had accomplished that but had also strengthened my mind so much so that I was now able to remember the events right after they happened. I later found out that I wasn't able to recall every abduction experience from then on, but I could a large number of them. Some I would remember more details about than others, still I would remember most of it.

I was taken so many times to the same room I had remembered that night. I eventually learned that this was a sort of "intake room" as I would call it. The place where they first take me and give me a brief exam before taking me to do whatever it was they had planned for me. Most of the time there were only three aliens there conducting the intake exam. Occasionally, there would be four of them, and at times one of the tall ones would be there, but that wasn't often. I was in my twenties when I first realized all of this. I would have conscious memories of these experiences simply surface, sometimes triggered by something I saw. At times, they would come back in lucid dreams, and as I previously stated I had started remembering the abductions experiences immediately after they happened. It all started making sense. With every abduction experience, I would put together another piece of the puzzle. I quit resisting them. I succumbed to the realization that there was nothing I could do to stop them. I felt it easier on me to co-operate and give them what they wanted. I just wanted to remember it all, the good, the bad, everything. I wanted some kind of control and that would be the only control I felt I had a chance of having.

I decided to take a course in hypnosis that was being given at a local metaphysical store. I felt I needed to make my mind as strong as I could in order to keep retaining my memories of the events. I also wanted to block the Greys from being able to hide these memories in my subconscious. I practiced the hypnosis techniques on a daily basis. I practiced on others, and I routinely did mental exercises on myself. I would subject myself to extreme conditions such as heat or cold. Then I would use self-hypnosis to convince my body that it wasn't feeling these effects of these conditions. I would take myself to faraway places in my mind. A technique I used quite effectively when I had to get cortisone shots into the heels of my feet for inflammation. The doctor was amazed at my lack of response to the pain of the injections. I got very good at strengthening the power of my mind. Soon I was able to use it on the Greys.

The small Greys are almost completely emotionless. They seem to have a thought process based on logic. I've often felt that the small Greys are all tapped into the same brain source since they all act and speak in much the same way. It's as if they are biological robots who are all programmed with the same software. Maybe they simply have some kind of "hive" mentality but that is the case none the less. On previous abductions, there had been times that I had noticed them seeming a bit confused and not knowing how to react to certain things I would say or do. I decided that the next time they took me that I was really going to cause them some confusion. When the time came I had ended up in the usual place they first took me too, the intake room. This time when I opened my eyes and realized I was having an experience I didn't panic. I did just the opposite. I closed my eyes again and started to use self-hypnosis to block their control of my mind. I heard a slight shuffling in the room. I felt ready. I didn't feel the usual paralysis through my body, but I continued to remain very still. I opened my eyes but didn't see any of them although I knew they were in the room with me. I heard one coming up on my left side. As the Grey came into my sight line, I suddenly rose up off the table and let out a spooky sort of little scream. The one closest to me who had been leaning over suddenly raised to a full standing position and took two or three steps back. There were three other Greys that had been a few feet behind that one. They too took a few steps backs. My actions were illogical to them. They didn't know how to react. They seemed confused as to what to do. They all just stood there gathered close together by the wall looking at me. I started to laugh. "I got you!" I yelled out. "What do you think now you Bastards?" I exclaimed! After all of the things they had done to me, I had finally if only for a few fleeting seconds, gained control. It was the greatest feeling. If they feel fear, then I had just scared them. If they don't feel fear, then at the very least I had sent them into mass confusion. They learned that night that my mind was stronger than they had ever estimated. A part of me would like to believe that it helped but there is a part of me that believes that it made them even more interested in me and caused them to do some very cruel and horrible mind experiments on me. Maybe they would have done them anyway; I have no way of knowing. They were testing my mind and my emotions. The mind games were about to begin.....

After pulling my big surprise in the intake room, I found that the tall Greys had now taken a much more avid interest in me. After my exam in the intake room, they gave me a garment to put on. The garment was a dark color and was made of some sort of fabric that would stretch to conform to your body. Although they may have also given me footwear, I have no memory of them doing so. Sometimes I was taken to see the tall one whom I had first met at age five during my first abduction. He was the one I felt the most comfortable with. It had gotten to a point with him to where I could ask him questions, and he would answer me. It almost seemed normal to communicate with him although I still didn't like to look at his eyes and would do my best to avoid that. I'm sure that he was quite aware of that, but he never spoke of it. This particular time I was taken to the tall Grey he greeted me cordially. The room was full of computer like equipment with walls of lights and screens. The images on the computer screens looked like holograms. There were two levels to this area. One level was about seven or eight inches higher than the other. I was taken to the higher level. "I have something I want you to see", the tall Grey said to me. "Come with me", he said as he walked toward one end of the room.

There was a series of screens there that were sitting at an angle that was facing the higher level of the room. We walked over about fifteen feet to these screens. He was to my left when we came to the screens. He looked at me and lifted his left hand toward a screen and said, "Observe". I turned my head toward the screen to see what it was he wanted me to see. It looked like scenes from a Sci-Fi movie about the end of the world. I saw destruction on a mass scale. There were large fires in cities; everything was burning. Smoke and fire was billowing from the skyscrapers. The sky was dark with soot and ashes. The streets were littered with dead bodies and smashed cars backed by fire and smoke. Then I saw great floods and tsunamis wiping out everything in their path. I took my eyes off the screen and looked in the direction of the tall Grey. Before I could say anything he communicates to me telepathically, "continue", he states. So, I looked back to the screen once again. This time they showed me nuclear bombs exploding in many large cities. Over and over they showed these horrific doomsday scenes. Finally, I had enough. I had figured out over time that the Greys were interested in two things about our species. Those two things are human emotion and human sexuality. I knew that they wanted me to react to the tragedies they were presenting to me on the screen, but I didn't react. In fact, they seemed to be very perplexed by my lack of emotional attachment to these scenes. I turned to the tall one and asked, "Why are you showing me this?" "This is what is going to happen to your planet in the future", he said. "Your species will destroy your planet", he continued. I realized he was telling me this to observe my reaction to these prophetic statements. "No!" "You're wrong", I exclaimed! "I know that you will never let this happen to Earth. You will stop us from doing this before it is too late." There was silence that seemed to go on for a couple of minutes. I wasn't sure what was happening or what the consequences of what I had said to him were going to be. He seemed to be rationalizing whether or not to continue with this "mind game". Then he finally spoke. "You are correct." "It is not in our best interest to let your kind destroy itself and your planet." I felt a slight sense of retribution. I had beaten them at their own game.

From what I had learned through all my metaphysical reading and learning I knew and understood the law of cause and effect. I understood the balance of the universe and how important that balance is to all that there is. My instincts told me that they too believed and understood these basic principles. The destruction of the Earth would have dire consequences for the entire universe. Not only would the Earth be destroyed but so would the natural balance of the universe because of it. So, of course it would not be in their best interest or any other alien race either. They merely wanted to monitor my emotional reaction and had created this end of the world scenes in order to gain a reaction from me. I wonder what they thought when they realized that their experiment on me had failed miserably.

Whatever they thought, it didn't deter them from trying again. In fact, for a while during this time in my life which was when I was still in my twenties, it seemed that they were more interested in the mental experiments than they were anything else. Oh sure, the medical and sexual procedures continued but it seemed to me that they were more interested in doing whatever they could to bring out any kind of emotional reaction from me that they could observe and monitor.

The next time I found myself in the presence of the tall leader they won the mind game. I was taken to the same area as I was before when they showed me the nightmarish scenes of death and destruction. This time I was once again taken to the level that was the slightly higher level. This area was not very big. I would estimate about 10 to 12 feet wide and about 20 feet across. There was a very large piece of material suspended from the wall some way. It looked like some kind of clear plastic and very similar to the smaller screens that was used to show me the images before only much bigger. It was maybe 6 to 7 feet high and at least 10 feet wide. I was asked to sit down. I said that I would prefer to stand, and he didn't object. He was wearing the same kind of light brown/tan clothing as I had seen him in before. He was standing near the large piece of plastic looking material. I took a few steps towards him and stopped only a few feet from him. He started communicating with me telepathically as was always the case. He told me that he knew that I had read about religions on Earth. "How do you know that?" I asked. He explained to me that they had put implants in me and had monitored me. He told me that sometimes they would have to move the implants from time to time. "Why do you do that to me?" "I don't like it. I am not an animal" I said back. He explained to me that it was necessary for their study of our species and that they did not mean to harm me by placing the implants in me. "Why do you have such an interest in the religions of your planet?" He asked me. "I want to know the truth", I answered. It then occurred to me that I had a once in a life time opportunity. I had a chance to ask an extraterrestrial species about their religion and beliefs. "May I ask you a question about religion?" I said. "Yes, you may", he answered in reply. I thought for a moment and then I asked, "Who is your God?" Without any hesitation, he turned to me and said, "We are all one with the one who is all." I was stunned by the simplicity and yet complexity of his answer. I smiled and spoke out loud. "Yes!" Yes!" I said. I was very pleased with his answer. So pleased that I felt no need to ask him anything else on the subject.

He then asked me again to sit down as he had something to show me. This time I complied with his wishes. There was a small bench like structure along the area where the room level raised. It was only about 18 inches off the floor. It was a hard material with no kind of padding. Like everything else on the ship, it too had smooth rounded edges. I walked over to the bench and sat down. I'm almost 6'4" and when I sat down on this bench like piece I felt like a giant. The tall one was still standing in the same spot to the left of the large plastic looking screen. Above him and the screen, I noticed a series of symbols going in a vertical line almost all the way across the room. It appeared that they were etched in to the wall some way. They looked similar to Egyptian hieroglyphics but were clearly not Egyptian. I assumed that this was their method of writing. I remember thinking to myself how I would love to know what it said.

The tall one then spoke to me saying, "On your planet you have a disease you call cancer." I wondered to myself just where this conversation was going. "Would you like to know the cure to this disease" he then asked? "Of course I would", I replied still wondering what this was about. Suddenly the large screen beside him lit up. Then, from the top, a mathematical equation started appearing. Line after line it continued seemingly on its own. When there were several lines of this very complicated formula on the screen it stopped as suddenly as it had begun. I don't know if it had been preprogrammed beforehand or if he wrote it telepathically in the same way that he spoke to me. It was as if the computer and the tall alien were somehow wired together and all it took to control the computer was his thoughts.

I sat in silence for a few seconds still amazed by what I had just witnessed. Then I asked him, "What is this?" "This is the formula for the cure to cancer", he replied. "You may take this back with you when you leave", the tall Grey solemnly stated. I felt a rush of adrenaline flow through my body upon hearing his reply! "Oh my God, They are actually going to give me the cure for cancer", I so foolishly believed. "Can you please give me something to write it down on?" I politely asked. His answer changed everything. "No, you must remember it", he said. I felt myself becoming agitated. "There is no way I can remember this" I exclaimed! "Please, I'm not good at math", I pleaded. Then he told me that it was time for me to go. I was so angry! "Wait!" "Wait!" I screamed out loud. "Just let me write it down" I asked again. It was all in vain. Two small Greys came up on each side of me and took me by my arms to escort me out. I remember looking back over my shoulder as I was leaving and trying to get one good last look at the formula with the hope that there would be some remote chance that I would retain and remember it. I must have gotten hard for them to control because right after that I blacked out. The event made such a strong impression in my psyche that I immediately remembered it the next morning. That's when it hit me that my extraterrestrial captors had won this round. I was set up. They wanted to monitor my emotions. They wanted to gauge my reaction to such a monumental piece of information. For all I know, it might not have even been the formula for the cure to cancer at all. They knew I wouldn't understand it. They could have put up any kind of complicated equation and I would have had no way of knowing what it really was. They got what they wanted; again....

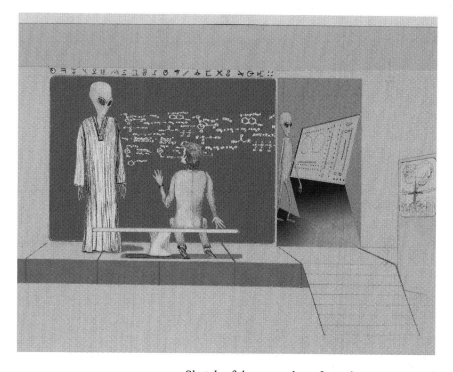

Sketch of the area where formula was presented
Copyright © 2013 Jeffrey Oldham

As the abductions increased so did my memories of them. Everything seemed to be happening at a very quick pace. I had also noticed that the paranormal activity around me was back and in full force. Occasionally I would hear the voice of yet another disembodied spirit trying to communicate with me. Sometimes I would talk to them. Sometimes I would ignore them. I was much more interested in learning how to stop these abductions than I was in ghosts trying to get my attention. Sometimes, if I would ignore their presence it would upset them.

One case in point happened at my parent's house in Las Vegas. I was sitting at the kitchen bar by myself. I had come to visit them when no one was home. I had a key to their house, so I let myself in, got a glass of water and sat down to wait on my parents to return home. They had a little black poodle named "Sam" who later became my dog. He was sitting at my feet. Sam had been in our family for several years and was a very intelligent, good mannered dog. Everything was quiet in the house. Suddenly, I heard movement in the hallway that lead out of the living room and den area to the bedrooms in the back of the house. "That's strange", I thought. I didn't get up to look because before I had the chance to Sam started looking in the area of the hallway entrance and began to growl as he got into a defensive stance. This really captured my attention as this was something that Sam rarely ever did. I had turned around in my bar stool to face the den area and the direction that Sam was looking in. I was looking all around the room for some sign of what was causing Sam to react in such a way. As I was doing this, I noticed footprint indentations in the thick carpet walking across the room towards me; one step, two steps, three, and then another. "What do you want with me?" I shouted! The footsteps kept coming. Sam backed up under me as far as he could. He was clearly scared of whatever it was that he saw. I watched as the footsteps walked by right in front of me not more than a couple of feet away. As it passed by me, an icy chill came over my body. This kind of chill had happened many times to me in the past when in close proximity of a ghost. This time was no different. As the footsteps passed by I heard a male voice say, "I'm here Bret." The footsteps continued into the pool table room. "Who are you?" "What do you want?" I called out in. There was no reply. I watched as the footsteps walked across the next room and walked right through the sliding glass door in the back of the house.

Apparently, there had been several strange occurrences in the house before that day. Several things had come up missing and unexplainable sounds and noises plus doors opening on their own and so forth. It all came to a climax not long after I saw the footsteps. My mother had slept in after my Dad had left for work when the entity, which we now know, was a dark entity, crawled into bed with her while she was sleeping. She woke up to what she described as someone trying to rape her. She felt the full weight of something on top of her and attempting to sexually assault her. She couldn't move, and for a minute she said she couldn't even scream. She could see nothing but felt the strength and force of the dark entity on her and the sound of heavy breathing. Finally, she was able to scream for help. Even her frantic screaming did not make the dark entity stop. I had taught her to call out to God and say spiritual affirmations in the name of God and make demands of the spirits/entities if ever the need came to do so. This was that time, and she did exactly what I had told her to do. After repeatedly screaming out these affirmations and prayers, she felt the weight lift from her and the movement stopped. The entity had left her. We always assumed this was the same entity that had made its presence known to me. Why it left me alone, I don't know. My parents stayed in that house for less than a year after that. My mother could never get over the fear of the entity returning and that awful experience happening again.

During the 1980's and into the 1990's the mind games would continue; with each abduction. Sometimes they would do their examination on me or whatever physical procedure they had in mind for me and then tell me to get dressed in the clothing they provided. Most of the time, I would co-operate and follow their orders. On one such night, I was escorted down a hall to where several of the tall Greys were standing. They were all dressed the same in the brownish tan robe looking uniforms and all of them looked very much the same with the same features. There was some size differential though which is not the case with the small Greys who all appear to be very close to the same height. There was a row of windows to my right that looked into a large empty room. I was taken into the room and left standing in the middle of it. I looked around and could see absolutely nothing. All of the tall ones and a few of the small Greys were standing at the row of windows looking in at me. "What are you doing?" I asked. There was no reply. I started to feel a bit anxious about what they were going to do to me.

"Will somebody please, just tell me what you want me to do?" I asked again, raising my voice this time. Once again there was no reply. I was looking at all of them standing in the windows like statues. There was no movement, no communication, nothing.

All of a sudden the whole scene changed. I hadn't moved from the place I was standing in, but now I wasn't standing in a room aboard an extraterrestrial spacecraft instead I was standing outside in a yard. It was a beautiful sunny day. The sky was clear and blue with just a few wondering clouds. The grass I was standing in was such a vibrant green. The trees were large and full of big green leaves. Everywhere I looked was filled with vivid, radiant colors that almost overwhelmed my senses. I could hear birds singing. I could also hear a small dog barking behind me. I turned around and was shocked to see my little dog Sam. The same Sam I mentioned previously. When my parents moved from the house with the entity they asked me if I would take Sam. I agreed to take him. Sam spent the remaining few years of his life with me until he passed at the age of 16. I really loved that dog as many of us do with their pets and I sorely missed his companionship.

I became so absorbed by my surroundings and the experience of seeing my little dog again that I completely lost touch with the reality of my situation. I knelt down to pet Sam. Joy filled every part of my being. Sam looked so young and full of energy just as he had in the prime of his life. He was so happy to see me too. His little tail didn't stop wagging as he jumped up on me and gave me kisses. I was petting him and hugging him. I was telling him how much I missed him as I played with him. It all seemed so very real. I didn't for a single moment even question what was happening. My emotions had taken over. I was so lost in the happiness of the moment that I had become oblivious to anything else. But, the cold hard bite of reality was about to rear its ugly head.

As I was still in a kneeling position and playing with what I perceived to be my beloved deceased dog, it all disappeared in an instant. I once again found myself in the empty room. The spot where I had been petting my dog was now just a cold barren floor. At first I was confused. I slowly raised my head up and looked around. I could see the aliens still standing on the other side of the windows staring in on me. I felt so foolish; I had fallen for their mind game and gave them exactly what they wanted, emotions. Then I became very upset for the mental cruelty they had induced on me. I knew they had gone into my memories and retrieved my memories of Sam. They had used them to create this scene. Whether they did it with some kind of sophisticated hologram or simply put the thoughts and images in my brain, I don't know. I do know that it was as real has anything I've ever experienced. To put me through that was more than I could handle. I became very angry and started shouting at them. I made threats. I called them names. I swore at them as I walked close to the windows. They never reacted to any of it. They stood motionless and observed it all; I was giving them more of what they wanted. They had hit pay dirt that night as my emotions ran the gamut. I do believe that they were in fear of me that night. I don't remember any of them coming into the room during my episode of anger. I don't remember anything else at all from that night. They must have had to subdue me in order to return me. The last thing I remember was still standing with my face close to the window screaming at the aliens on the other side of the window as they all stood with those same blank expressions on their faces.

They must have gotten a lot of data from that particular experiment on that night because they decided to do it again. In January of 1986, my Step Father passed away from lung cancer at the young age of 46. He was the man who raised me and the only Dad I had ever known growing up. It was a huge loss to my family and had deeply affected all of us. It was that deep emotional scar on my consciousness that my extraterrestrial tormentors had decided to use this time.

During this abduction, I found myself being led once again to the empty room with the large windows. I hadn't forgotten what they had done to me the last time I was in that room. They placed me in about the same spot as I had stood on the previous occasion. The others had gathered outside the windows just as they did before. As the two small Greys who led me into the room exited, I raised my voice. "You're crazy if you think I'm going to fall for this shit again!" I yelled at them. As usual, I got no response, either verbally or physically. I felt the familiar sense of frustration that I often would have during the abductions of not being able to evoke any sort of emotional response from my alien captors. I felt like a dog who was begging for food but being ignored by his masters. Perhaps they remained silent on purpose to provoke more emotion from me that they could observe and monitor. I had come to understand their fascination with our human behaviors. I knew it was something their race of beings had lost somewhere through the genetic changes of generations. Maybe they never had it at all, but it was obvious that they wanted to learn about what part of our genetic makeup caused these emotions to surface. They would stop at nothing in order to evoke them.

I was determined to resist these holographic images that I knew that I was about to experience. "Concentrate." I told myself. "This isn't real." I kept repeating over and over. I closed my eyes in the hopes that I wouldn't see what was happening. Then I heard a familiar voice say my name. "Bret." He said. He continued, "What are you doing?" It was the voice of my Step Dad who had passed. I did what anyone would do under the circumstances. I opened my eyes and there standing six feet away in front of me was someone who looked like my Step Dad. As with what happened with my dog on the previous experience, we were standing outside on a grassy area. This time though I didn't notice the sounds of nature as I did before. Maybe the Greys made a mistake and forgot to add that minute detail. It didn't matter whether the nature sounds were there or not. The visual images I was experiencing were very real to me. It was so easy to fall into the false reality the Greys had created. My Step Dad was wearing blue jeans and had no shirt on as was often the way he would dress when relaxing at home or outside in the yard. He was younger than when he died and looked to be in his mid-thirties. I'm sure the Greys had pulled this image straight from my conscious memories of him as well as the tone and dialect of his voice. They did a masterful job.

I knew I shouldn't have, but I spoke to him. "It's so good to see you Dad." I said to him. "I've missed you." I continued. "I've missed you too" he replied. He stepped closer to me and gave me a hug which caught me by surprise. My Step Dad was a very kind and caring man, but he was never a very affectionate man, and that isn't something that he normally would have done. The Greys had made a mistake in having him do this. I know they were trying to see my reaction to this loving gesture, but it brought my mind back to the reality of what was really happening to me. I didn't make much of an effort to hug back of which the image of my Step Dad didn't seem to notice. He was looking at me and kept smiling. He was a very handsome man and had a wonderful smile still he would never just keep smiling like that, no matter how happy he was. The Greys had made another mistake. That was all I needed to break the hold of this illusion. "Where are we Dad?" I asked him. "How did we get here?" I then asked. He didn't reply. I stepped back further away from him. "You're not real, you're dead!" I shouted. I continued, "You're not really here", "You're not real!" It was then that I could see the whole scene vanish. To this day I still have vivid memories of watching the image of my deceased Step Father standing there looking at me as he simply vanished. I remember feeling so lonely and empty inside as the whole thing ended. This time it was me who was standing motionless with a blank stare on my face. I felt numb. They had inflicted pain on me many times before; physical pain which would eventually end. This time it was different. The cruelty of what they had just subjected me to inflicted a pain that would last forever.

# Chapter 5

# We Want Your Sex

As I opened my eyes all I could see was an intense bright white light. I began to panic. I tried to move, but as usual, the only part of my body I could move was my head. I frantically looked around to get some bearing of where I was. I could hear movement in the room with me. It sounded like people shuffling around. I raised my head up as far as I could and still couldn't see anything. The light was right on top of me and engulfed everything in my range of vision. I closed my eyes again somehow believing that it would all be gone when I reopened them. When I did opened my eyes again, it was all still going on. I really began to freak out. Then the bright light above me was slowly pulled away from being directly on top of me to down towards my thighs. As my eyes adjusted I could see them; three tall Greys and a couple of smaller ones in the room with me. One of the tall ones came up beside me on my left side. He never spoke but somehow his presence evoked a sense of peace and tranquility over me. He stood about a foot from me with his hand slightly raised in a position with his palm facing me.

I then turned my attention to the other Greys in the room. The other two tall ones were at the foot of the table I was laying on. I looked down the table at them, and I noticed that I had no clothes on. "Where are my clothes?" I asked. No one answered. I was fifteen years old at the time. My familiarity with these extraterrestrial creatures had long been instilled in my subconscious. I wouldn't remember them during my everyday life, but when I was taken there was a strange sense of knowing what would happen. My instincts told me that they were about to experiment on me again. This time it was different. "We want to make you feel good", said the tall one next to me; as usual, not speaking to me verbally in the literal sense but telepathically. I was very confused. Making me feel good was not something they normally did.

Then two small Greys rolled over some kind of machine. It had an arm on it that protruded out and looked somewhat like a small crane; on the end of it there was a round cylindrical object about 8 or 9 inches long. It would remind one of a metallic test tube only with a larger circumference. My legs were spread open in a fashion similar to a woman's position during a gynecological exam. They began to bring the tubular piece closer to my penis. "Stop!" I shouted. The tall Greys beside me told me to relax. "This is something we need to do. It won't hurt you. This, you will enjoy", he said. All of a sudden my head began to fill with sexual thoughts. I was young, curious, and my hormones were in full capacity. I had these kinds of thoughts before. Everyone has sexual fantasies at one time or another, but this time these fantasies seemed real. It felt like I was really experiencing the fantasy. I had gotten an erection. I couldn't help it.

When I did, one of the tall Greys took the cylindrical object and placed it over my now erect penis. The sensation the device produced was like nothing I had ever felt. The pleasure it gave was beyond words. I was brought to an intense orgasm. Upon which, they immediately removed the device from my penis and rolled the machine away. I felt exhausted even though I hadn't done anything. The aliens all began to leave the room. They turned off the bright light. There was now only a soft dim light in the room. I could now move my body but had no desire to at this point. I remained motionless. As the euphoria of the event begun to wear off, I tried to cope mentally with what had just happened. I was young and didn't understand at that time why they would do such a thing to me. I felt violated. I felt raped! I was getting angry. I rose up and placed my hands down on the examining table on either side of me. I didn't know for sure what I was going to do. I only knew I was going to get some answers. But I never got the chance. As I turned to get off the examining table, I blacked out. There must have been one of them in the room with me monitoring my every move and probably my every thought. He saw to it that I would go no further than the table. That's the last thing I remember of that night.

That was the first time they took sperm from me but far from the last. I would endure this procedure many times over the course of my life. Yes, it would still feel good, but as time passed and I came to expect what was about to happen, I would mentally put up resistance to the point that it would dull the sensation. I believe that a big part of the pleasurable feeling derived from the device was instilled psychically from the Greys. When I resisted it would affect the feeling, but I could never stop them even though I tried. It all became very routine. I felt like an animal in a lab. To them, I'm sure I've never been much more than that. They got what they wanted and needed from me with no regard as to what damage it would do to their unwilling victim.

As the memories of these sexual events surfaced it had a profound psychological effect on me; I had been taken against my will. I had been held prisoner. I had been forced into sexual servitude. All of this and I couldn't tell a soul. I had never felt so alone in all my life. I was suffering, and I had no recourse. I would sympathize when I would hear a story of a woman being raped. I understood her emotional trauma. I too had been raped. In my case, I was raped repeatedly, over and over through the years. I had been violated and used. I struggled with self- worth. At times I would feel that I was nothing more than a biological experiment of these strange insect looking creatures from another world. Other times I would try and make myself feel special by attempting to convince myself that there was something unique about me that the aliens liked. I told myself that this was the reason they would not leave me alone. I surmised that I had something very special about me that appealed to them, so they kept coming back for more. Who knows? Maybe in some way that was the case. Maybe there was something in my DNA code that they were looking for. That's something that I may never know for sure. They've never told me. They just keep coming back, time after time.

It is very humiliating to write this chapter, but I am willing to endure it. I feel it is imperative to reveal what must be told about these extraterrestrial beings and what they have subjected me to. I'm sure there are hundreds, if not thousands, of other abductees holding in these same kinds of deep dark secrets just as I did for so many years. I'm sure there will be those who will make fun of me and talk about me behind my back. I can accept that. People mock and ridicule what they fear and don't understand. The truth has to be told about what is really going on. Many psychologists have stated that the whole abduction phenomenon is stemmed as a direct result from repressed childhood sexual abuse. I will state right here on record that I strongly disagree with that hypothesis! Yes, there is a sexual aspect to this because that is part of the Greys agenda. I can't accept the sexual abuse rational any more than I can for sleep paralysis or lucid dreaming being blamed. The abduction phenomenon is much bigger and goes much deeper than those easy out diagnosis. I know without a shadow of a doubt that I was never sexually abused by a human being during my childhood. That is not what this is all about. Any scientist, doctor or psychologist who so easily dismisses what is really happening in these abduction scenarios is making a huge mistake.

The taking of my sperm was not the only sexual procedure done to me during my abductions. The Greys are extremely interested in all areas of human sexuality. They not only want to understand the emotional aspects of it but the psychological and physiological aspects as well. They are and have conducted experiments on our human population in relation to this entire spectrum of studies. I have memories of being an unwilling participate in two of these bizarre experiments.

I had been in the intake room and given the usual exam by three of the small Greys. I was in my mid-twenties and by this time in my life I had stopped most resistance on my part. In the end I knew it would just be another futile attempt. I had begun to cooperate with them for almost everything they did to me. I only had asked them to not let me feel any physical pain from any procedures they did on me to which they would often oblige. Upon completion of this exam during this particular abduction one of them came up close to my head and spoke telepathically. "Get up and follow me", he commanded. "Where are we going?" I asked. There was the usual silence. The small Greys would rarely answer me. If I ever got an answer to any of my questions, it would usually come from a tall Grey. The tall one whom I had first been introduced to would provide me with most of my answers, but even he had his limits. It was clearly evident that there were limits as to what I was allowed to know.

I followed the small Grey as I was instructed. Two other small ones followed behind me. I was completely nude and yet somehow it didn't feel awkward. We walked down a small hallway and turned left into a very large dome shaped room. I can only describe it as having the shape of an eggshell cut in half. There was a long ramp to our left that ran along the side of the room. The ceiling was high; maybe a couple of stories high. I had never been in this part of the ship before nor had I ever seen a room this large in their craft. In the middle of the room, the floor was sunken. There was small mattress like structures lined up across the floor.

The mattresses were only four or five inches thick and were placed directly on the floor. They had a blue material on them similar to what I had seen on other benches and such in their craft. At the top of the ramp, there was a large platform that over looked the entire room. There were cutout shapes that raised up off the floor of the platform that were being used as seating for the Greys. The platform floor and seating looked to be all one giant piece. Everything had a smooth edge to it much like other areas I had seen in the craft. A tall Grey wearing a brown tight fitting uniform was sitting in the middle seat. There were two other tall ones sitting on each side of him. Several small aliens were standing in back of the tall ones. I was escorted higher up the ramp. I saw two rooms toward the top of the ramp. There were no doors on either room. When we approached the first room, I hesitated so I could look in. The lighting was a bit dimmer in the room but still bright enough to see clearly. The room was small. I was shocked to see the room stuffed full of naked men. Some were sitting on a small bench that was protruding out from the wall. The others were standing. It looked like a crowded subway car. There was no room for these men to move. I immediately noticed that all of the men seemed to be in a trance like state. They had their eyes open but were catatonic and completely oblivious to me and even the others in the room with them. The Greys coaxed me on. Before I walked on, something else caught my attention; I noticed that all of the men in the room had dark hair.

I wanted to ask why those men were in there, but before I had the chance to ask, we came upon another small room. It was exactly like the room I saw the nude men in but this particular room was full of naked women. I tried to stop at this room also. The Greys wouldn't let me stop at this room. I quickly observed that the women in this room also appeared to be in a trance induced state and were just sitting and standing motionless exactly like the men were. None of them seemed to notice us passing by the door to their room. Like the men, they too didn't appear to be aware of the other women in the room with them even though they were all standing or sitting shoulder to shoulder.

I was walked to the large platform. I knew that some kind of experiment was going to happen. I also knew that I was going to be a part of it whether I wanted to or not much like the other human captives that were there with me that night. I've never understood why I hadn't been put into the same trance like state as the others. I was brought over to the tall Grey leader. Even though they all look so similar, I was able to recognize him as the one who had been communicating with me since the beginning of these abduction experiences. I believe that they are able to create a psychic bond between each other and also between us and them. It wasn't so much that I was able physically to recognize him as the one who had been around me from the beginning; it was more of a strong inner feeling about it. He spoke to me in his usual kind and articulate manner. Unfortunately, I don't remember what it was he said to me that night. I only remember standing there beside him as the smaller Greys began to bring out the men and women from the two rooms I had looked into.

They all proceeded in an orderly fashion to the floor below the platform. Everyone seemed to be under complete mind control. No one appeared to care about anyone else in the room. Never mind the fact that everyone was totally nude. None of the humans looked afraid of the aliens either. It was all very precise and orderly. Just as the Greys liked it as I had learned. Everything had to be organized and logical. That is the way their thought process works.

The platform at the front of this room was 8 to 10 feet higher than the floor where all the blue colored mattresses were on. There was a small set of stairs protruding from the platform that would take you down to the area where the mattresses were. I watched as the small Greys meticulously placed their human subjects exactly where they wanted them. They took all the women and assigned a mattress area to them. I'm assuming that the women were instructed to lie down as that is what they all started doing. No one spoke. No one resisted or even attempted to resist. They willingly obeyed every command from their captors. All the men were placed beside a blue mattress and remained standing. I noticed that even though there was a room full of naked women lying on these mattresses before them, none of the men were looking at the women. They were all standing with their heads up and looking forward. Soon I was now being escorted down to the floor. Even though I wanted to resist I couldn't. My mind was thinking it yet my body wouldn't follow. Now they had a lock on me too. I wanted to speak out but couldn't. I wanted to stop walking but couldn't. I felt like I was on remote control and I didn't have the controller. They took me to the fourth row back and placed me beside at the foot of the mattress of the second one over.

The women were just lying there acting as if they were in a drug induced stupor. I had my gaze lifted to the tall leader who sat in the middle seating area. It was like a zombie army, and I was a part of it. The tall Grey leader sat there for a minute or so with his long spindly arms up on the ledges of the seating area looking like a king in his throne. No one in the room was moving. Not even the other Greys. He raised his left arm up and gestured towards us. At that time, all the men in the room began to get on top the women. It happened to me also. It didn't matter whether I wanted to or not as I'm sure was the case with everyone else in the room that night. It was mind control beyond being simply hypnotized. There was no way to stop it. Suddenly I was aroused. I had no idea how or why this would happen. I looked down at the dark haired women on the mattress. She made no eye contact with me but did not try to stop anything that was transpiring. I began to have sex with this stranger. It was like my body was a machine and I was inside of it. I had absolutely no control over my body. I felt a strange sort of separation from myself. Everyone in the room were all doing the same thing; the men on top of the women in a standard missionary position. It wasn't some kind of wild sexual orgy by any sense of the imagination.

After a few minutes, I was told to stop, which I did. I was told to stand up which I also obeyed. I was then directed to a different woman two rows up from where I had been. I noticed some of the people were still having sex. Others were changing partners as I was instructed to do. Oddly enough, the second woman they put me with looked very similar to the first one except younger. I wondered if they hadn't been a part of the same family. I'm sure there was some kind of purpose to it; something that these alien beings wanted to observe or needed. As I walked to the second woman, I looked up at the platform. All of the aliens were watching intently; not moving at all. They seemed to have a very strong interest in the mechanics of their experiment. I really don't believe they received any kind of sexual gratification from it. They are extremely fascinated with human sexuality, and this was one of the ways they observed it. It was under their control, their rules. In this way, they could watch and match up whom they wanted to. I didn't think about it then, but I've often wondered if the women were being impregnated that night only to later have the fetus taken by the Greys. The whole process seemed very well planned. I believe that there is a good chance that everyone there was handpicked because of their DNA code. Maybe that's why all the men had dark hair and from what I could tell so did all the women I saw. I've always wanted to know if the others involved in the event that night were feeling the same thing inside that I was. Did they know what was happening to them as I did? Did they have the same overwhelming feeling of helplessness? Did they too feel like nothing more than a lab rat in some mad scientist psychotic experiment? I went for years worrying that someday I would meet one of the unwilling participants from that night and that they would recognize me from being there or perhaps I was the only one whose memories had surfaced. Many times I wondered if any of them ever remembered any of it. For their sake, I hope not.

The taking of my sperm would continue for years. There were times that they would take it more than once in a night. I'm sure to them that was the logical thing to do. They had me so why not take as much as possible while they had the opportunity to do so. Surprisingly enough, I never questioned them as to what they were using it for. I questioned the procedure, but I never asked them what they were using my sperm for. I assumed that it must be a part of their study of human anatomy. I later found out just how wrong I was, and it would be the Greys who would show me.

I was first introduced to a hybrid alien during another one of their sexual procedures. A hybrid alien, in this case, being both human and Grey: a hybrid mix of both species. This event happened when I was in my mid-twenties. Up until then, I had only seen two types of these extraterrestrial beings on board their craft, the tall leaders and the small worker Greys, and I had seen other humans but never a combination of the two. I remember feeling very subdued and relaxed during this particular abduction. I didn't resist anything as they once again looked me over after my arrival. I felt numb to it all. I was going to let them do what they were going to do. I didn't speak nor did they. It was the usual cold, sterile environment, devoid of anything remotely resembling feeling or emotion. After I was poked, prodded and scanned with instruments, two of them coaxed me up from the table. I didn't know where it was they wanted me to go, but I knew they wanted me to come with them to another part of the ship. I felt a bit groggy almost zombie like. I walked along in a haze. Not really observing things on the craft as I normally did.

We turned to my right and entered a room I had never seen or been in before. It was very barren except for a sofa/ bed piece of furniture in the middle of the room with the same blue colored material on it that I had seen several times before on furniture like objects in the ship. There was another small room inside the room that was enclosed with darkened windows. It was in the corner of the larger room, about 20 feet behind the piece of furniture. I couldn't see into it, so I have no idea if it was occupied or not. Once again I was walking around their ship in the nude. They had made no attempt to cloth me. In my state of mind that night, it made no matter to me. I didn't care. I didn't care about anything at that time. They took me over and sat me down on the blue sofa bed and then left the room. I was very puzzled by it all. "Where did they go? What is it that they want me to do?" I asked myself. Nothing could have prepared me for the answer to that.

I was facing the middle of the room. The entrance to this room was behind me and to my left. From my peripheral vision of my left eye, I saw movement. Someone was entering the room. I quickly turned my head around to see who it was that was approaching me. "Oh my God", I whispered out loud. The visitor entering the room was alien, but unlike any alien I had ever seen before. It had long white hair, so I assumed it was female. She had much smaller eyes that looked grayish in color. She was frail and tiny but not as small as the small Grays I was used to dealing with. She gracefully walked over to me and sat down across from me on the sofa bed. Time seemed to stand still as we both stared at each other. I realized that I was looking at my first hybrid. A flurry of emotions rushed through my body like a raging river. I didn't know how to react. I didn't know what to say. I just sat there completely oblivious to the fact that I was sitting there across from this female alien hybrid in the nude. It was shocking and yet it was all starting to make sense to me at the same time. All those times they had taken sperm from me, all the sexual experiments and observations they did. The result and the reason was sitting right in front me, staring at me with the same curiosity that I had about her.

I felt no fear as I looked at her and yet I still never attempted to communicate with her. It was all so overwhelming that it had left me speechless. She was wearing a very loose fitting white colored garment much like the nightgowns women use here except the fabric looked more like a thin, wispy nylon sort of material. To my surprise she suddenly reached down and pulled it up over her head and removed it. She never changed her expression after removing her garment. She just kept staring at me with this peaceful look on her face that was actually pleasant to see. Even though, she was now also nude, I felt a sense of comfort with her. I looked at her body. She looked thin but humanlike. Her breasts were small but looked very much like a human woman's. She had her right leg folded back on the sofa bed, and the other dangling down the side of the sofa bed but she was turned enough towards me that I could see she had no pubic hair. Other than the hair on her head she appeared to me completely devoid of hair. Her feet and hands looked very similar to a human's except that her fingers were a bit longer and more slender than most humans are. She really wasn't the hideous creature one might think something like this would be. I certainly wasn't attracted to her, but I wasn't appalled by her either.

Then without any warning, I hear a voice in my head! "We want you to mate with her", the voice says. The voice continues, "That is why we brought her here", it explains. I speak out loud," I will not!" I shout. The female hybrid seems to know that I am being spoken to. She must have known what was being said because she moved closer to me and wrapped her arms around me. Her skin felt different than the Greys but not quite like ours either. Her hair brushed up against my face as she tried to get next to me. I had both arms to my side and was attempting to slide back away from her. I was not sexually aroused at all, but I got the impression that she was going to try and mount me. I knew from past experiences that they somehow can make me aroused when they wanted to and that there was nothing I could do to stop it. I worried that they would do this again at any time. I didn't want to hurt her in any way, but I wanted her to stop, so I reached up and grabbed her around her tiny waist and pushed her back away from me. I looked at her, and for some reason I felt compelled to apologize. "I'm sorry. I can't do this", I said to her. To this day I have no idea what happened after that. Either they did something to me, or I have subconsciously blocked that memory from my mind. I think it's better that I don't remember what happened next because I know that the Greys usually get their way. Sometimes the truth is better left alone.

# Chapter 6

# The Gift

Fall has always been my favorite time of the year. The heat of those long summer days is subsiding. There is a fresh crispness to the autumn air. Leaves turn many bright and brilliant colors painting a rich canvas. I've always felt a new energy in the fall season. Maybe it all stems from my youth, back when I played sports. I participated in several sports. Basketball was my main sport and October was not only the beginning of autumn and Halloween, but also the beginning of basketball season.

Every new season I would look forward to getting my yearly sports physical. Yes! Strange as it sounds I actually enjoyed them. The reason was I knew I was extremely healthy. I knew that I would pass my physical with flying colors just as I had always done. My health was something I had taken for granted for a very long time. I was never sick, and I really never gave it a second thought as to why that was. Sure, I would get an occasional sinus infection or a sore throat, but even those were rare. The mysterious illness that came on me when I was fourteen was really the only major illness I had ever had growing up. To this day, I still remain very healthy.

As with many things that had to do with my alien abductions, I didn't realize just why it was that I had been so healthy all my life until I got older. After my "awakening" that realization and many others came to light. I knew that these alien visitors who have repeatedly visited and taken me my entire life had indeed interacted in order to keep me strong and healthy. One could argue with some validity that I am simply blessed genetically and yet that argument merely opens up a whole myriad of other possibilities and theories. Such as, maybe the aliens have been altering my family's genetics for generations. I have been told that my Great Grandfather Lewis on my Mother's side was never sick a day in his life. He also had a strong energy flow like me and was often hired to dowse to find water for wells. Like many other alien abduction researchers, I believe that once the Greys find the genetic traits that they prefer, they will continue to use that particular individual. They sometimes will also take other immediate family members. This can go on for generations. There is no way to know exactly how they have kept me this healthy or even if it is something to do with the DNA of my family. What I do know is that there have been far too many incidents throughout my life to chalk it up as mere coincidence.

Before my memories began to surface of my abductions, I had already begun to suspect something was very odd about certain physical abnormalities. I had been told by a couple of different doctors that I have a rare blood type. What that blood type is I don't know as I was never told anything other than it is rare.

Several times I've been accused of cheating while taking the standard eye exam of reading the letters on the chart. I would zip right through the line they would ask me to read and then continue on to the next line down. I wasn't supposed to be able to see that line. No one should have been able to. So the nurse or whoever was giving the eye exam would ask me if I had memorized the line before the test started. I don't think any of them ever believed me when I would tell them that I didn't. I thought it was kind of fun when I was younger, but as I got older I was insulted by such comments.

The same type of thing happened to me when my ears got plugged one time when I was nineteen years old. I went to the doctor for it, and they irrigated my ears. Apparently, there had been a wax build up which the ear irrigation cleaned. Afterwards, they asked me if I had ever taken a hearing test to which I replied I had not. The doctor suggested I do one and asked the nurse to administer the test to me. She took me into a different room, and I sat down at a table. She explained the test to me which was simple. I was told to hold my hand up when I heard a tone. At first the test seemed to be going along fine. Then I raised my hand when I heard a certain tone. "Why did you raise your hand?" The nurse asked. "I heard a tone", I replied. She looked at me funny and wrote something down. The test continued and then the same thing happened. "Did you hear that one?" The nurse asked me. "Yes", I said innocently; completely unaware of what was really transpiring. She made some more notes and continues the test. Again I raised my hand after hearing a tone. This time the nurse got angry. "Ok!" She exclaimed. "You need to stop playing around. This is serious stuff we are trying to do here, and you should take it as such". I took the test equipment out of my ears and laid it on the table. I was quite perplexed by her reaction. "I'm doing it exactly what you asked me to do", I told her. I continued, "I'm not playing around at all." When she saw I was being truthful she explained, "You were raising your hand on tones that humans aren't supposed to be able to hear. I don't know how you possibly can hear them". She asked if I would do the test one more time to which I agreed. The results were the same. She was flabbergasted and remarked to me as I was leaving how the doctor wasn't going to believe this one. I am in no way suggesting or claiming to have some kind of super human abilities. The only explanation I have is that the Greys were responsible. Whatever they did served me well but didn't last. I still have very good hearing, but years of playing guitar in rock bands have diminished my hearing somewhat. My eyesight was always so good that I never thought that I ever would have to wear glasses, but I do wear them now to read so whatever they did, either they removed it on purpose, or it didn't last.

I've had many medical anomalies over the years that neither I nor anyone else can rationally explain. Sometimes I had been mysteriously healed. Sometimes I was left with scars from the procedures that they had done on me. It seems some of the medical procedures that they done on me were for my benefit. A part of me would like to believe that, but deep down in my heart of hearts I know it's most likely not the case. Keeping me healthy benefited them as much as it did me. They were using me. They needed me to stay healthy and saw to it that I always was.

Although, there were other times that I believe I came back with an affliction from them. In the mid 1980's, I had one of these strange incidents happen. One morning I woke up feeling like I hadn't been to sleep the night before. This is a very common feeling the morning after an abduction. I can only describe it as feeling as if your entire body is full of lead. It is extreme tiredness. It's almost like being awake and on the go for two or three days. It's all you can do to muster up the strength to function for the day. I had no conscious memories of anything happening to me the night before, but by then I knew what was and had been happening to me, so I suspected an event had happened. My suspicions were confirmed as I got dressed. As I was putting on my underwear, I noticed a large red mark on the upper left side of my groin. It was about the size of a silver dollar in circumference. I thought that maybe I was allergic to something that I didn't know of and had a reaction to it causing me to develop what I believed to be a rash. It didn't itch or hurt, so I wasn't too concerned at that point. I figured that I would get some ointment for it, and it would be gone in a couple of days. And that's exactly what I did but not only did it not go away, it got worse. The rash had started to spread. All kinds of thoughts went through my mind. I needed to stop this stuff before it spread any-more, so I made an appointment with a local dermatologist whose office was close to my work.

I arrived at the dermatologist office and filled out the paperwork. I wondered what kinds of questions he was going to ask me of which I had no answer. I couldn't dare tell him where I believed I had caught this weird skin condition. I decided just to play dumb; just go through the motions, get some medicine and get out of there as quickly as possible. Well, I soon found out that my plan wasn't going to work. The nurse came in and started with all the questions. "Does it itch?" She asked. "No, not at all", I replied. That was an easy one I thought. "Do you have any allergies to anything?" The nurse then asked. "Not that I know of", I replied back. Then she dropped the big one, "Have you been exposed to any poisonous or unknown chemicals or sub-stances?" I felt flustered. I hesitated; I didn't know how to answer that one. Finally, I said, "I'm not sure". The nurse then asked to see the rash. I pulled my pants down enough to show her the area con-taining the rash. From the look on her face, I could tell she didn't have a clue as to what it was. She asked me to leave the rash area exposed and told me the doctor would be in soon.

By now, my curiosity was really up. I tried to reassure myself that the doctor would know what it was. After all, she was just the nurse. The doctor had a lot more education and probably more experience. After I had spent a few minutes anxiously waiting for the doctor, he finally entered the room. After exchanging pleasantries, he asked me most of the same questions the nurse had. Then the doctor said, "Let's take a quick look at it and see what we have going on here". He leaned over and looked at the mysterious rash for a bit. Then grabbed a large light and used it to look at the rash again. All the while he remained silent. Finally, he says, "I don't believe I've ever seen anything like this before. I want to take a small sample and test it". Of course, I agreed. I was now getting quite alarmed at the situation.

He left and came back with a small tray containing various medical instruments. I'm not sure what all he did. When I looked down he was taking a small scalpel and scraping a piece of my skin off where the rash was. He placed it on a slide and left the room. A few minutes later he came back in and took another sample. "You can pull your pants back up now", he said as he left the room again. I sat there on the examining table feeling very confused. All kinds of thoughts raced through my mind as to what I had. Questions like how serious it was. Was it going to keep growing and take over my body? Was it contagious and if so would I have to be isolated? I thought lots of crazy stuff. Finally, after what felt like an eternity the doctor and the nurse came back in. The doctor looked down at my chart for a few seconds. He then raised his head and said to me, "I'm going to be honest with you Bret; I still have no idea what it is we are dealing with here. You're welcome to get a second opinion if you want, but there's not a lot I can do for you at this point". I was stunned! "Is there anything you can give me for it?" I asked. "I'll give you some cream to apply to it, and we'll hope for the best", he replied.

I used the cream the dermatologist gave me for a couple of weeks just as the directions indicated, and it didn't work. The rash didn't go away but at least it wasn't getting any bigger. I was beginning to believe that this unusual rash was going to be permanent. A couple more weeks went by, and I considered going to see another dermatologist, but I've never had much faith in doctors, so I never did follow through with it. Eventually, the rash began to disappear. It took a few months for it to disappear completely. I was so relieved when it did and just chalked it up to another one of those weird anomalies that happened to me.

Oddly enough, every few years after that I would get the same rash in the same area for no known or explainable reason. I never tried to do anything to get rid of it as it always eventually went away on its own. I had even gone to the library and researched on my own hoping to find a clue as to what this reoccurring skin condition was and how I got it. I never found anything in any of the books that looked like it. I knew then why the doctor had no idea what it was. It wasn't in any medical books!

In 2001, I got the rash again. This time it was different. Not only had it reappeared in exactly the same spot on the left side of my groin area as it had before but now there was a spot on the right side of my groin area in direct proportion to where it was on my left side. This time I got very worried. I had never had it this bad before. I had pretty much assumed by 2001 time that the rashes I kept getting were caused by something I was exposed to on board the craft during one of my abduction experiences. It was the only explanation that made any sense and also the one I couldn't tell anyone. I didn't know what to do. Once again, I thought about going to see another dermatologist. "It's been several years. Maybe they have something for it by now", I tried to convince myself. I decide to wait and see if this time the rash would go away on its own as it had done all the times before.

After a week or so there was still no change in the condition of the rash. I tried to think of some alternative medicine that might work. I got the idea to go to the China Town area of Las Vegas and look for something in their herb shop that might help. The Chinese herb shop was very busy. I waited my turn to ask for help. I tried my best to explain to the man behind the counter what I needed. His English was broken, but he got the basic gist of what I was saying. He walked my over to an area of the store and said something to the effect of wanting to see the rash. That wasn't going to happen! I tried to explain to him where it was at, and he nodded his head as if he understood. He pointed to a small tin container and told me that it was what I needed. I figured I had nothing to lose but a few dollars, so I bought it. I was willing to try anything if I thought it had the slightest chance of working to eliminate the rash. I tried to read the ingredients of the small tin container but couldn't since I don't read Chinese.

When I got home I opened the small red tin container and applied some of the thick white cream to the rash. The cream wouldn't soak into my skin very well and would cover the rash turning into a white paste as it dried. I used the Chinese cream religiously. At first nothing happened but then I started to notice the rash decreasing in size. Maybe it was disappearing on its own like all the other times except that this time it seemed to be doing it at a much faster pace. I believed the cream from the Chinese herb shop was working. The rash did indeed quickly disappear with no trace of it ever having been there. It has only returned once since then, about a year or so later. Again it was my left side. I used the Chinese herbal cream immediately, and the rash didn't last long. I've never had it again since then. Whatever was in that small tin container healed the strange skin condition. Although I have no memory of it, I have wondered if I might have complained to the Greys about the rash their equipment or some chemical they were using was giving me. Maybe they changed something to prevent it from happening again but then again, probably not......

Living in the hot arid desert of Las Vegas, Nevada one is exposed to many days of sunshine. While that in and of itself can be a good thing, especially for outdoor activities, it can have unfortunate health ramifications also. One of the negative aspects of so much constant sun exposure is skin cancer. I have a dark complexion with an olive colored skin tone. I rarely ever get sunburned so in the years prior to the public education of the harmful rays of the sun and their relation to skin cancer, I never wore any kind of sunscreen. There were many days I spent boating on Lake Mead without anything on but my swim trunks. Other days I would be playing tennis or basketball with my shirt off, all the while getting constant exposure to the sun. Eventually, these harmful habits caught up with me. I began to notice more and more small moles developing on my body; especially on my upper torso. It finally got to the point that I decided that I had better go to a dermatologist to have them looked at, which I did. Fortunately for me, it turned out to be nothing serious. The doctor simply burned most of them off. Although it was a painful procedure, I was still relieved that no cancerous moles were found.

I began to be more aware of how much I was exposing my skin to the hot Vegas sun after that and I would use sun screen on a regular basis, but the damage had already been done. A few years later, which was sometime around 1991 to 1992, I noticed a few more moles popping up on various areas of my body. One in particular had really caught my attention. It was on the left side of my upper chest area. It seemed to come out of nowhere and had grown to about the size of a dime. It was discolored and had an irregular shape. I had looked at photos of skin cancer, and it looked like what I had seen in the photos.

I was working at my family owned air conditioning and appliance business at the time. Shortly after arriving one morning I waited until no one was around and told my Mom about the mole that looked cancerous. She asked to see it, so I pulled up my shirt and let her take a look at it. She agreed that it looked like skin cancer and suggested I call and get an appointment to see a doctor right away. I took her advice and called that day to make an appointment with the same dermatologist that had burned off my other moles a few years prior. The dermatologist's office was very busy, and I couldn't get in for a few days. I made the appointment and figured that a few more days wouldn't make that much of a difference anyway. I felt a sense of relief now that I had went ahead and made an appointment to see a doctor and get this mole taken care of before it got too serious. I went ahead with my day of work and never gave much more thought to the problem.

The next day was just another normal work day and then things got strange. Very strange! As I was getting dressed on the third day after I had made my doctor appointment, I happened to notice something that sent shockwaves throughout my body. The cancerous looking mole was gone; completely gone! There wasn't a trace of it left. It was as if it had never been there. I couldn't believe it! I rushed into the bathroom. I wanted to get a better look at it in the bathroom mirror under the bright lights. The result was the same. Nothing, there was no mole anymore.

I got dressed and headed off to work. I couldn't wait to get there and show my Mom what had happened. I was still in disbelief and trying my best to rationalizing what happened. As soon as I walked in the door at work I said to my Mom, "I want you to take another look at that mole I showed you before". "Is it already getting worse?" She asked. I wanted to see what she was going to say when she saw it, so I didn't reply. I got under a light and pulled up my shirt for her to take a look. "Where is it?" She asked. "It's gone. I woke up this morning, and it had disappeared", I replied. "What do you mean it just disappeared? How can that be? Moles don't just disappear on their own" she exclaimed! I lowered my voice to a whisper so no one else could hear. I told her that the only thing I could think that happened was that the aliens had got me again and had removed the mole. She was one of the few people that I had told about some of my alien abduction experiences. We both agreed that that was the only way it could have disappeared so quickly. I asked her not to tell anyone about it and then called to cancel my appointment with the dermatologist.

I really don't how the timing of it worked out unless the aliens were monitoring me at that particular time and knew I was con-cerned about this mole being skin cancer, so they took me and removed it. Why wouldn't they have just let the doctor remove it? I don't know. Maybe it just so happened that they were going to take me anyway and when they did they too noticed it during my examination. Or maybe, they removed it to demonstrate to me that they cared for my well being or was it in their best interest to keep me healthy, and that's why they helped me? Whatever the case was, this cancerous looking mole I had got removed and my good health continued. This is the paradox of my abduction experiences. They have hurt me and yet they have helped me.....

One of the most difficult aspects to deal with from being a vic-tim of these alien abduction events is the psychological damage that is done from the whole abduction experience/s. I repeat this statement throughout this book like a mantra for good reason. I want people to know that this phenomenon is real and what serious damage it causes to the unwilling participates chosen by these alien beings. I believe that everyone that has gone through one of these abduction events has been left with psychological scars. Most abductees have no memory of what has happened to them. They are the lucky ones and yet too many of them look for causes for their various emotional and mental problems elsewhere; never suspecting or knowing the real underlying cause. Those of us that do have memories of what has been done to us still don't have much recourse. We deal with the fear of humiliation if someone finds out about it. We are afraid to seek professional help for fear we will be considered crazy, delusional, having hallucinations, schizophrenic or any of the other numerous psychotic illnesses they would come up with. I'm sure some doctors would question whether illegal drugs were being taken. We don't know whom to trust or where to seek out help. It is a heavy burden to carry.

Those of us who have been taken against our will by these obtrusive extra-terrestrials have not only been left with psychological scars, but many of us have also been left with physical scars stemming from the procedures done to us during the abduction/s. As I mentioned in an earlier chapter, I am one who has some of these unexplainable scars on my body. I have no conscious memory of how I got any of them. I do know that there has been nothing in my life that has happened to me here on earth that can explain any of them. I've only ever had one surgery, which was for a hernia in my groin, and that was in 2012. Besides that surgery, I've only had stitches twice, once in my jaw and once in my forehead. I have scars from both accidents that caused those cuts, and I clearly remember how and where they came from. I can't say the same about the other scars on my body.

As I wrote about in a previous chapter, my Mom had first noticed a large mysterious scar across my lower back during my teen years. I was fourteen at the time. She had called our family doctor and was told that it was probably stretch marks and was nothing to worry about since they were common in young boys. Even though the doctor had told my Mother over the phone what he believed was the cause of the scar, he never examined me in person. Still yet, I had readily accepted the doctor's diagnosis.

After the discovery of the first scar, I started paying closer attention to my body and over the years I have gotten into the habit of turning around and looking at my back and other hard to see areas of my body, in the bathroom mirror after showering. During one of these times, while I was drying off after a shower and looking at my upper torso and back, I noticed two more unusual scars. These scars were much different from the one on my lower back. While the scar on my lower back is in a straight-line horizontal formation, the new ones I found looked like round puncture marks. I still have all of these scars. The circular puncture marks are on my left side down several inches from my arm pit. They are in very close proximity of each other but slightly different looking in texture, formation and size. The smaller one is approximately a 1/4 inch in diameter and appears more rounded than the larger one which is approximately 3/8 of an inch in diameter. I was just as curious about these two new scars I had discovered as I was the one on my back, but I never told anyone about them at the time. Before when my back scar was reported to a doctor I was told it was something natural. I wasn't about to make another call or visit to a doctor for what I thought would again be something easily explained, so I decided to keep quiet about it.

Puncture mark scars on upper left side torso

I went through my teen years fully accepting the explanation the doctor had given my Mom about the large scar on my back. Eventually, I quit looking at my scars and didn't give it much thought until my "awakening". It was then that I started to suspect the real origin of these strange marks left on my body. By chance one day during a doctor visit to another dermatologist, I got quite a shock. I don't remember my exact age at the time, but it was during the time I had begun to realize the truth of these abduction experiences and what had been happening to me.

This time I had went to a dermatologist because I had a break out of acne. He asked me if I had any acne breakouts on any other parts of my body. I had told him that sometimes I would occasionally have some problems on my shoulders. He asked me to take my shirt off and to lie face down on the examining, which I did. He began to examine my back. "This is nothing to worry about. We can easily take care of it", he stated. The next thing he said took me by surprise. "Where did you get this scar? Surgery?" He inquired. I could tell by the tone in his voice that he was quite curious about the scar. "I've never had surgery", I replied; which at that time was true. "That's odd. This looks like a surgical scar", he replied. He continued, "If this isn't a surgical scar then how did you get it?" He asked. "I don't know. I thought it was stretch marks", I answered. "No, I don't believe this is stretch marks. I've never seen any stretch marks that look like this. This is very strange. Very, very strange", he said as his voice trailed off. As I was putting my shirt back on he asked me how long I had the scar, and I told him. He was still shaking his head as he said his goodbye and left the room.

A couple years later, also in the early 1980's I was working at night as a full time musician and working a full time job in the day time as a delivery driver for a local television and appliance store in Las Vegas. This was back in the day when all the televisions were still the heavy tube type, so I got quite a workout every day frequently lifting the TV's. Eventually, I hurt my back and went to see a chiropractor to see if he could help. He didn't have the x-ray machine in his office than most chiropractors do these days, so he sent me to a nearby hospital that he worked with to get my back x-rayed so he could determine the extent of my injury. After I had taken several x-rays, the x-ray technician told me to wait a few minutes. He was in another room looking at my x-rays when he yelled out to me. He asked me how long ago it was that I had my back surgery. This was all getting to be too much. I told him just as I had told the dermatologist that I had never had back surgery. He started to argue with me about it and rather emphatically insisted that I must not have remembered it but that my x-rays clearly showed that there had been work done on my lower back and even named the vertebrae area of my spine as to where it was at. I don't remember the exact area he named, but I remember at the time knowing that it coincided with the area of the large scar I have. He even went so far as to explain more medical details about what he saw, but I really didn't understand what he was talking about nor did I really want to believe him. I listened and played along with him until I left.

Photo of large scar on my lower back across my spine

Close up of the large scar on my lower back across my spine

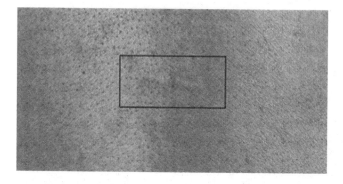

Photo of one of the smaller scars, Approx. 1.1/2" long, near my spine
in the mid torso area of my back

I knew I had an unusual scar on my lower back. For years, I had thought that it was the result of stretch marks. I also knew that I most definitely had never had surgery on my back. When the doctor first asked me about the scars, was when I started to suspect that I must have gotten them from some alien experiment or procedure. When the x-ray tech was so adamant about seeing the results of surgery to my spine I was convinced that they, (the Greys) had indeed done some surgical procedure to me in that area of my spine. Years later more scars would appear on my back. These are smaller scars and higher up my back close to the mid torso area. To this day I have no idea exactly where or how I got these mysterious scars on my back and the puncture type scars on my side upper torso area.

I have tried many times to figure it out, to make sense of it. Whatever happened must have been so painful that no matter how hard I try to remember I can't. My subconscious must be protecting me from reliving this horrible event that caused the scars. I have accepted it and yet a part of me still clings to the hope that they are stretch marks, but I know that if they are then they are different from any stretch marks I have ever been able to find and compare them to. They are also different from scars left by back surgery so if they are indeed surgical scars then it was a surgery done in a very different way than the way surgeons here use. I can't explain them nor can I explain the puncture marks other than to relinquish it all to the obvious, aliens. Oddly enough, in the subsequent years following that earlier back x-ray, I have since had my spine x-rayed again and no one has ever mentioned seeing anything that would indicate back surgery having been done previously. Maybe they saw it and didn't say anything or maybe a second procedure was done to me which healed the initial problem. I am only speculating here but whatever the case; the scars remain. It would be many years later as part of my paranormal research that I may have gotten the long sought after answer.

My wife Gina and I do a lot of research and experimentation with the ITC phenomenon. ITC communication, which stands for (Instrumental Trans Communication), is a means of spirit communication using what is commonly known as a "ghost box" or a "spirit box". We use a regular Am/Fm radio with the scan mechanism disengaged so the radio will continually scan. One can achieve spirit communication this way as the spirits will use the white noise between radio stations as an energy source to speak. Nikola Tesla, the famed inventor, and whom I believe to be one of the greatest minds in mankind's history, first developed this. Tesla stated publically that not only was he receiving communication from what he perceived as spirits but that he was also getting what he believed was alien communication, all through radio waves. Gina and I have had amazing results with ITC work, as well; which I will go into more detail about in a later chapter. We've had thousands of answers from the spirit world during our many spirit box sessions. Some of which are very profound.

During one particular session we were doing, we decided that if Tesla spoke to spirits and also claimed to be getting responses from what he believed were alien life forms, then we should also try to communicate with aliens. It was a long shot. We knew our chances of success were slim, but it was worth a try. We were at the home of our good friend and fellow paranormal researcher, Sandy Nichols, who is also an abductee. Sandy and I both knew that we had been implanted during our abductions with what we believe are tracking devices that also monitor us. Sandy and I talked about it and thought it was logical that the Greys would know that we were attempting to communicate with them through these radio frequencies by monitoring our implants. If so, then maybe there was a chance that they would speak to us through the spirit box. We did receive some very interesting replies, but of course there is no way to know for sure who or what was replying. However, I was getting enough answers to satisfy me that whoever was replying sure seemed to know a lot about my abduction experiences and so I asked, "Why did you do surgery on my back that left these scars?" I got a quick reply back in a voice that seemed devoid of emotion and human tone. "It was for life", they said. I was stunned! My Mom had first noticed the scars after I had been very sick with the mysterious illness and then had suddenly gotten well. Had the Greys actually healed me by performing some kind of surgery on me? Though all the agonizing and painful things that they had done to me over the years, had they at one time also given me the greatest gift of all, life.

# Chapter 7

# The Baby Takers

I opened my eyes to the bright sunlight shooting through my bedroom windows filling the room with the radiance of a beautiful morning. I rose up and sat on the side of the bed. I felt groggy. It was one of "those" feelings. The kind of feeling I have after they have taken me. I took a couple of deep breaths and tried to collect my thoughts. I didn't remember anything unusual happening during the night before. I didn't even remember having any dreams. Nothing was unusual except for having this feeling like I had never gotten any sleep that night. As I started to stand up to get dressed, I happen to look back at my pillow and got quite a shock. Red blotches smattered all over the white pillowcase. Blood stains! My pillow had blood stains all over it! I quickly ran to the bathroom to look for any cuts. I found no cuts, but when I blew my nose I noticed dried blood. My nose had been bleeding that night. It was then that I knew they had taken me once again. That explained the familiar groggy feeling I had. I assumed that they had implanted me again or removed the implant that they had previously placed up into my nasal passages. I had experienced nosebleeds before off and on throughout my life, but this was 1988 and by this time I knew what was causing them, and it wasn't the arid air of the dessert. That night began a period of heavy alien abduction activity for me, and strangely enough paranormal activity too.

For several months following the morning of finding the blood stains on my pillowcase, I had a problem of getting these unprovoked and quite random heavy nosebleeds. This had happened to me before at other times during my life, and now they were back. These nose bleeds came out of nowhere and often at the most inopportune times. I remember one of my old friends from high school coming out to visit Las Vegas during this time. I hadn't seen him in years. We spoke on the phone and agreed that we would go to dinner and then I would take him to see the sights of the Las Vegas strip. I invited my girlfriend and together we picked my friend up at the Hilton hotel on Paradise road where he was staying. We had a great time at dinner recollecting about the old days back in school. After dinner, we took him down the famous Las Vegas strip and had stopped in the Riviera hotel and casino. We were on the floor of the casino in an area of several slot machines. We were walking through the casino and talking along the way when I felt a trickle of blood come out of my nose. I touched it with my hand and verified that my nose had started bleeding. I asked a casino attendant for a tissue, but before the attendant could hand me a tissue my nose started bleeding profusely. I made a dash to the rest-room to get some paper towels. After several minutes of attempting to stop my nosebleed, I gave up. I exited the restroom, apologized to my friend and left. I wasn't able to drive so I asked my girlfriend to drive home. The nose bleed was so bad that I considered going to the hospital. I eventually got the bleeding to stop after I got home.

Unfortunately, this kind of incident had become commonplace for me by then. I never went to the doctor for the nosebleeds after I got older. I had been before for the same problem when I was younger, and they had found nothing wrong. I knew what the cause was. I just didn't know how to stop the Greys from doing the procedures on me that caused the nose bleeds. During other periods of my life, the succession of chronic nosebleeds would cease on their own. I figured that this time would be no different and that I eventually would get back to normal after a few weeks of having to deal with the problem. When I was young, I had been taught by a doctor, a couple of medical techniques to use in order to slow or stop the bleeding. I had learned to handle these small emergencies with aplomb. To me, it was a minor inconvenience compared to some of the other experiments and medical procedures that my alien captors had subjected me to. It seemed during periods of frequent abduction activity that these uncontrollable nosebleeds always occurred. It was another consequence of the abductions that I had learned to deal with. During the years of 1988 and 1989, I would experience new consequences that I would have to learn to deal with. Even then, I could have never imagined just how difficult that would be.

I met noted UFO researcher John Lear during this same time when all of these abduction events had begun to escalate. John was doing public presentations speaking about UFO's and alien abductions at various locations throughout the Las Vegas valley. It really piqued my interest when I heard about one of them, and I decided to go. The event was held in a large room at the Spring Valley library on South Jones Boulevard in Las Vegas. When I arrived and entered the room where his presentation was being held I was surprised to see such an impressive turn out. John drew a large crowd of what appeared to be very interested UFO enthusiasts who listened and responded with enthusiasm to John's every word. I too was very impressed. John was clearly intelligent, sincere and very knowledgeable about the subject of UFO's and aliens. This was the first time in my life that I felt a certain kinship with others who seemed to have likeminded beliefs as mine. My entire life was spent experiencing these repeated alien abductions, and I never felt comfortable enough to talk about it. I knew I had to meet John and learn more. During his presentation, I noticed that when someone from the audience asked him a question it was difficult for the audience to hear them due to the size of the auditorium. So after, his presentation was over I approached him to meet him and to offer my help. I was in a band at the time, and we owned sound equipment, which included wireless microphones. I told John how much I enjoyed his presentation. John was and still is a very cordial man. We chatted for a few minutes about UFO's and then I offered to help him with the sound the next time he did a speaking engagement. We exchanged phone numbers.

I really wasn't sure if I would ever get a call from John, but sure enough, he did call me the next time he had a presentation. He offered to pay for the use of the sound system which I refused. The singer in my band, his girlfriend and my girlfriend all helped. It all worked out great! My singer and I ran the sound board, and the ladies went through the audience with the microphones to hand to whoever had a question.

John was pleased with how smooth the event went and thanked us all for our contributions to the success of his presentation. Afterwards, he invited me and Tad (the singer in my band) up to his house to visit. We readily accepted John's gracious invitation. I remember really looking forward to it and hoping that I could learn even more about the UFO phenomenon and especially the alien abductions that John had spoken about since he had focused mostly on abductions by the Greys. At that time, there was absolutely no one except maybe two or three family members that knew anything about my abductions and I'm not sure what they thought about it. It was just one of those things that was never really discussed. Maybe they didn't want to hurt my feelings. Maybe they just thought it would pass or maybe they simply didn't know what to say. I know they respected me and believed that I was telling them the truth. I never expected them so say much. I mean, what could they say? Even I couldn't understand it all, and I was the one experiencing it. I saw John as a ray of hope in all this. Maybe he knew what I could do to stop this atrocity that was being administered to me. I knew I needed help, and I needed it right then.

I was very interested in what John had learned from his research. His background and aviation accomplishments are nothing short of incredible. I knew that his research was thorough and well thought out. John was from a well known family and had a lot to lose by going public with what he knew. I respected that and admired him for his fortitude and willingness to take that kind of risk. I was intrigued by the thought of what else he might know that he wasn't revealing to the public and hoping that he would share some of it with me. I would not be disappointed!

My first visit to John's house was both comforting and inspirational to me. Tad had decided to accompany me to John's house that afternoon. Tad had become interested in the UFO subject after listening to John's presentation and wanted to learn more. John was very welcoming upon our arrival and invited Tad and me into his large first floor den. The walls were lined with photos and commendations of John's illustrious career as a pilot. John holds several world aviation records. John's father Bill Lear was the inventor of 8 track tapes and also designed the Lear jet. It was apparent that John had been exposed and inundated with the aviation industry from an early age, and it showed. John's accomplishments in the field were and still are very impressive. It was a glorious afternoon. As the minutes ticked away, I felt more and more comfortable talking to John. I began to ask one question after another and to each John would do his best to answer. Sometimes he would pull out certain papers to show us. Sometimes he showed us videos that he had obtained.

It was like pouring water on a sponge. I absorbed it all and hungered to learn more. I felt the more that I could learn about these various extraterrestrial life forms visiting our planet then the more power I had against them or at least in the ones who were taking me. The things I was learning from John went deeper than the usual "flying saucer" stories I had read before. This was real! In your face real! Although I did touch upon the subject of alien abduction on that first afternoon, I didn't heavily pursue it. Nor did I dare reveal my own personal abduction secret yet. After spending a few house hours talking, reading and watching UFO related matters, Tad and I left with our heads spinning from all the fascinating information that John had so unselfishly shared with us.

A couple of weeks later I got a call from John. He asked me to come over to take a look at some new information that he had received. I was more than happy to do so. This time I went by myself and once again spent several hours talking to John; especially about the alien abduction phenomenon. The conversation centered on the Greys and the large number of people who were coming forward with their own alien abduction stories about them. This was the first time in my life that I had something to compare my experiences to. Yes, I had seen other humans in their spacecraft before, but I had never heard any of their accounts as to what had been done to them. In a strange sort of way, I felt comforted in learning about others who had these same kinds of experiences as I had. I felt a sense of belonging and a bond with these people although I didn't know any of them.

I knew I wasn't alone in remembering the harrowing accounts of being taken by these strange mysterious creatures from another world. I found similarities and certain patterns in the Greys behavior, in not only what they did to me, but what they did to others, as well. John told me about Bud Hopkins and his work with the victims of alien abduction. He recommended me reading some of his work about the subject. John didn't directly ask me then, but I'm sure he must have suspected that I too was one of these unfortunate victims.

I did heed John's advice and bought one of Bud Hopkins's books. I'm not sure which book of his it was "Intruders" or "Missing Time", but I wasn't able to read very much it. It would emotionally affect me. The more I read, the more those feelings of fear and dread would come to the surface. I would find myself becoming depressed. I would have trouble sleeping for fear that this would be the night that the Greys once again would return to take me. I could talk about the subject of alien abductions with John. I could even watch a short piece about it on a television show, but if I spent too much time reading about it then for some reason it would affect me. Later I would experience the same thing while attempting to read Whitley Strieber's very popular book "Communion". I tried a few years ago to read John Mack's book "Abduction". Although I managed make it through a few chapters on "Abduction", I had to stop reading that one also. It was just too depressing.

To this day I have never read an entire book about alien abductions. I have even had to take several breaks away from writing this book because of the emotional toll it was taking on me to relive and recount my own personal abduction experiences. Writing this book has been both liberating and psychologically exhausting at the same time. I have been able to watch movies and speak with others about the subject of alien abductions, but even that will sometimes bring those painful memories back that it seems will forever haunt me.

As the weeks and months passed my friendship and trust of John grew; I finally revealed to him that I too had suffered from and experienced these alien abductions from the Greys. John didn't seem the least bit surprised. As any good researcher would do, he began to inquire about it. Probing for more information and what all I remembered. I recalled several accounts of my experiences to John. One afternoon, he brought in his wife Marilee and had me tell her about one particular experience. Marilee was very cordial. She asked several questions about the encounter I had told her about and even took some notes. I could never tell if she believed me or not. She did seem to have a genuine interest although nowhere near the interest that John had. That was the only time I ever remember her being in on any of mine and John's conversions about UFO's and aliens.

It was sometime during this time period that John met the famed Area 51 whistle blower, Bob Lazar, whose name has now become synonymous with Area 51 in the Nevada desert. Bob Lazar is a physicist who claimed to have worked on a classified government project named Galileo, which he claimed consisted of back engineering alien spacecraft. He also claimed to have received a 2 page briefing document in which it stated that alien life forms did indeed exist, had been integrated into human evolution and that their spacecraft were being kept at an area known as S4. This area was 15 miles away from Area 51, deep within Papoose Lake. Lazar said that there was a complex there that was built into the bottom of the Papoose Range that had nine aircraft style hangar doors all angled at 60 degrees. He even went so far as to draw diagrams of the saucer shaped alien craft. Lazar described the space craft that he worked on as being powered through an anti-matter reactor and a yet unknown energy source at that time named Element 151.

John contacted a well known award winning news journalist/UFO researcher, George Knapp, with this information and the story broke. A media firestorm soon erupted over the entire thing. Yes, this was profound news, to say the least. I have seen Bob Lazar in person but have never met the man. John was convinced that Bob was telling the truth and during a recent interview I did with John that was published in the May, 2011 issue of Alternate Perceptions magazine, John revealed that he does still keep in contact with Bob Lazar and does still unequivocally believe him. There are many theories and opinions among ufologists about Bob Lazar. I've always found his story to be plausible. Living in Las Vegas, you come across many people with stories about Area 51. Most of which are very easy to distinguish the truth in.

One only has to go to You Tube to find video after video of supposed evidence from Area 51. There's even footage claiming it is of a captured Grey that was reportedly taken there after the famed crash of a UFO in Roswell, New Mexico in 1947. I've also heard of death bed confessions that do verify many of the claims made about the Area 51, the Groom Lake region and what goes on there. I've heard stories about a flying saucer crashing near Lake Mead, which was too big to transport, so it was simply buried. There are numerous UFO sightings reported by people from all walks of life around Southern Nevada. Something was at one time going on at Area 51, but I doubt that it is anymore. Whether or not any of it has or had anything to do with extraterrestrial races and alien space craft, is something that I seriously doubt the general public will ever know.

One of the most intriguing aspects of the whole Bob Lazar story was his claim in 1989 of a stable form of element 115. His critics came down hard on him at the time since element 115 had not yet been discovered. Many called him a fraud and the disinformation spread like a wild fire. Of course, this is often the case within the UFO community. There was a point when John Lear himself was being talked about as "working for the government" and spreading disinformation. This was easy to do for whoever was attempting to discredit John's claims since John had indeed once flown missions for the CIA. In February 2004 both Bob Lazar and John Lear had the last laugh when scientists were able to reproduce an isotope of element 115 in a laboratory. Furthermore, Lazar's claim that element 115 was formed in massive stars has also now been substantiated with recent advances in astronomy. I have to commend George Knapp for having the nerve to break a story like this. To this day, George is still involved in UFO research and is well respected for his work and research. These aforementioned men probably aren't aware to what degree of inspiration they are to others in the UFO field that are also searching for the truth and with the burning desire to get that truth revealed.

The high strangeness had escalated to a boiling point. Things were moving fast. Through it all, I was learning much about my experiences. In earlier chapters of this book, I wrote about some of my many paranormal experiences throughout my life and how I believe without a doubt that these increased paranormal experiences are a direct result from my alien abductions. My research and my personal experiences with both have led me to believe that there is a direct correlation between these events. I believe that my abduction experiences are inter-dimensional. These alien creatures have somehow mastered the ability to traverse between dimensions and quite possibly, time. This is why I feel that the vibration rate of energy in my body has increased due to them taking me through these dimensional portals and that this increase results in ghosts/ spirits being able to more easily see me or sense my presence more than the average person. So naturally they are drawn to me because of that. I have often stated that I feel that I am a paranormal magnet. It took me years to understand why and to grasp the concept of inter-dimensional travel. Once I did understand, I felt much more comfortable with my paranormal experiences. I now consider it a blessing that I attract these lost souls. My wife Gina and I will always do what we can in order to help them.

During times of frequent abductions it has always seemed like the paranormal activity around me would substantially increase. During this period of the late 1980's this premise held true. I was living with my girlfriend at the time. To protect her privacy, I will not use her real name here and will refer to her as Denise. At first, we started noticing objects being moved around the house. We always tried to find a logical explanation when this would happen, but we really never could so we just ignored it and carried on about our business. Then objects began to disappear. Sure, one might think that we simply lost or misplaced these things and at first that is also what we thought, but it became more and more frequent. Then things like the silverware started disappearing and sometimes other dishes. We began to lose so much silverware that it became very noticeable that we simply hadn't misplaced our eating utensils. Even stranger, one day we found some of it again piled up against the wall in our bedroom floor! Sometimes in the middle of the night, some unseen force would shake our bed so hard that it would wake us up thinking we were experiencing an earthquake. As soon as we would awaken it would stop.

It got to the point that we decided to bring in a psychic to go through our house and see what they could sense as being the cause. We asked a psychic who was a friend of my mother's to come over to help. We told her of the paranormal activity that was occurring and let her go through the house. She told us that she felt something of a negative nature there but never went to far as to say it was an entity. She said she couldn't quite put her finger on it so to speak. The psychic did focus in on an old flower vase that we had, and said she felt the paranormal activity may have something to do with this object. She felt that getting rid of the vase would stop the ghostly activity. I had read about spirits being attached to certain objects, but I didn't understand why one would be attached to an old flower vase. It was worth a try though so the next day we threw the old flower vase in a dumpster behind a store. We came back wondering if it could be that simple. We found out it wasn't!

For a couple of days, it seemed that getting rid of the old vase had worked. Everything was quiet. No more missing silverware or any other objects around the house. No more mysterious bed shaking in the middle of the night. Then something new began to happen. One night I set the heater at a certain temperature before going to bed. That night we both woke up noticing how hot it was. Uncomfortably hot. When I got up to go check the heater, I found it turned up all the way to the highest setting possible. I really didn't suspect anything paranormal. I figured that I must have inadvertently hit it as I was changing the settings before going to bed. I reset the heater to the temperature I wanted and then went back to bed. Nothing else happened that night. The heater continued to work properly during the remainder of that night and also all through the next day; we didn't think much more about it.

The next night I went again to turn down the heat before going to bed. I set the thermostat a bit lower and double checked that I had it at the temperature I wanted. That night we once again both woke up in a sweat. It was burning hot in the house! I got up to go check the thermostat and found the dial set to the highest temperature setting there was. I knew that this time I hadn't hit it. I reset it and stood there for a few minutes to see if it would stay on the setting. It stayed right where I had set it. I took off the cover and inspected it. I couldn't find anything wrong. I replaced the cover and went back to bed. A couple hours later we once again felt extreme heat and once again I got up to find the thermostat setting moved up. The next day we discussed what could be causing the thermostat to malfunction like it was. We even considered that maybe vibrations from 18 wheelers passing by on a nearby road were causing the lever to move. This was not a digital thermostat so maybe the little lever was moving from the vibration somehow. The problem with that was that the thermostat was always working during the day and lots of big trucks passed by during the day. I decided to call a repairman to see if he could find something. Maybe the thermostat was defective. That made the most sense to me. A repairman showed up and thoroughly inspected our thermostat. He couldn't find anything wrong with it. "It's working just fine". He stated. He continued, "Why did you think it was not working?" He asked. When we told him what had been happening, he wrinkled his brow and with a little half smile on his face just shook his head in what seemed to be disbelief. After he left, I still wasn't convinced that he was correct in his diagnosis. Something had to be causing it to change settings, and I was going to find out.

I got the idea to set the thermostat and then tape it with masking tape so that nothing would be able to move the lever to change the setting. That night I placed a couple of strips of masking tape over the lever after I set it to keep it from physically moving. Later that night it happened again. I woke up feeling the heat that filled the house. I sat up in bed with an uneasy feeling. I knew I had taped the lever on the thermostat so how could it have possibly been moved I thought to myself. "Didn't you tape the thermostat control?" My girlfriend asked. "Yes", I replied. I knew she could hear the apprehension in my voice. I knew I had to get up and go reset the thermostat, and I was a little uneasy as to what I would find. I went into the hallway where the thermostat control was at and flipped on the light switch. Although I was several feet away when I did, I could still see that both pieces of tape had been lifted off on one side of the control lever. I was stunned! "The tape looks like it's been moved", I yelled back to my girlfriend in the bedroom. "Come look at this", I exclaimed! Neither one of us could figure out how the tape could have moved. Now we were convinced that something paranormal was happening. Who or what it was we had no idea. That was now the big question. I don't think either of us got much sleep that night.

I had placed the tape back on the thermostat before we returned to bed that night and had left it on during the next day. The evening of the next day we had planned on attending a sporting event. Before we left I took more masking tape, and after setting the proper temperature on the thermostat, I encased the entire thermostat enclosure in masking tape. I thought to myself that now there is no way the control will be altered. It was an extreme measure to take, but at the time I didn't know what to do about the situation. I remember joking about it as we were leaving that night. It turned out that the joke was on me.

When we returned home that night I was in a good mood as I pulled in the driveway. We had a good time at the game and were talking as we walked up to the front door. I had forgotten about placing all the extra masking tape on the thermostat. I placed the key in the deadbolt lock and unlocked the door. As I opened the door to enter the house, I felt a rush of hot air hit me like a blast from a furnace. We had left a light on in the house and from the front door I could see down the hall where the thermostat was. "What the Hell", I exclaimed! I hadn't yet stepped inside the house, but I knew something was wrong. I could see something lying on the floor in the hallway under the thermostat. I slowly walked toward the hall to get a better look. My girlfriend was right behind me and too freaked out to speak. As I walked closer, I could clearly see it. I felt a rush of adrenalin fill my veins. "This can't be. It's impossible", I told my girlfriend. There, scattered on the floor beneath the thermostat was the masking tape I had placed around it. It was scattered everywhere and had been torn into tiny little pieces. No masking tape had been left on the thermostat itself. The heat had been turned up all the way again. That was it! We decided right then and there that we were moving. Something unseen didn't want us there, and we were happy to oblige. We called the landlord the next day and told him we moving because the place was haunted. I had experienced spirit contact many times in my life before but nothing as malevolent as this. This felt dark. It felt negative. It was time to leave in the hopes that it would be appeased. We wanted peace and we needed rest. We ended up getting neither.

We found another house right away. Everything at the new house was fine for the first few weeks. Nothing strange or paranormal was happening. The energy felt light and not as oppressive as the house before. I felt like whatever was bothering us at the other house had indeed stayed there. Denise and I both were relieved that the strange events had stopped; things were back to normal for awhile. Then one day when I came home from work Denise said we needed to talk and asked me to sit down. "I have something very important to tell you", she said. I could tell that something was wrong. The first thought that entered my mind was that she had experienced something paranormal. "Is it back? Did something happen again", I asked her. "No, no, nothing like that". She replied. "I think I'm pregnant", she suddenly blurted out! As you can imagine, this came as quite a shock to me. Denise had been taking birth control pills, so she was just as shocked as I was to learn that she had gotten pregnant. "Are you sure?", I asked. My mind was racing. I was trying to comprehend the seriousness of the situation and at the same time trying to understand how this happened with her using what is normally a very effective method of birth control. "I'm pretty sure, but I need to go to my gynecologist to make sure", she answered. I didn't know what to say. I don't think she did either. "Well, let's find out for sure, and we'll go from there", I told her and reassured her that it was going to be OK.

Denise made the doctor appointment for the next week. I went with her to the appointment. Her doctor asked her if she had quit taking her birth control pills. She told him that she hadn't until she thought she might be pregnant and then she stopped. He said that it was rare but that sometimes women do get pregnant while on birth control pills. We learned that day that Denise was indeed pregnant and that she was close to 3 months into the pregnancy. I don't think either of us was really ready for that kind of news. We knew we had some big decisions to make. We started making plans when we decided to keep the baby.

Not long after we had confirmed Denise's pregnancy, I started experiencing signs of abductions again. I had told Denise about my abductions by the Greys, but I never went into any real details. I had explained to her that it was too painful for me to talk about. She said she understood and never asked any further questions. I'm sure she was very curious and wanted to know more, but she respected my wishes not to talk about it. I had told her that someday I would explain and that when I did she would understand how difficult it was for me to dredge up those old memories. I remember telling her that the Greys weren't these little friendly aliens being depicted so much in the media. She appeared perplexed by that statement. Denise did once ask me if I was afraid of them; to which I answered an emphatic "Yes"! She knew me well enough to know that I wasn't afraid of much. I could tell that she was alarmed by my reply and left it at that without pursuing it any further. Denise had a similar interest in the UFO subject and had accompanied me to a couple of seminars and other UFO related events. Even though, we often talked about various things we had heard or learned at the UFO seminars, she would never bring up my own alien abduction experiences.

One morning I woke up before her, and I knew something was wrong; my body felt paralyzed. I started to panic. I knew I was wide awake. I could see the walls and ceiling of the bedroom. The bright sunlight shot through the window and filled the room. With my peripheral vision, I could see Denise still sleeping beside me, so I knew I wasn't dreaming. This was reality, and I couldn't move! Try as I might, I couldn't move a muscle. I had that sense of dread, of heaviness that happens after 'they" have taken me. I realized the way I was feeling at that moment was exactly the same way I would feel many times while on their craft especially during certain medical and even sexual procedures done on me by the Greys. I knew that this effect was still the residual mind control that they had used on me. This method is used by the Greys as a way to subdue the individual they are taking. Do I believe that they really paralyze you? No, I don't at all, as pertaining to the real physical sense, but if your mind believes that you can't move then you won't be able to move. I cannot stress enough the power of the mental abilities of the creatures. They are very frail as a physical specimen, but their intelligence and ability to transform thoughts to us is beyond our human comprehension. The human race would be rendered completely defenseless against this particular species of alien beings should we ever have any sort of confrontation with them. They easily would win without a single weapon being used except their own minds.

Once I recognized these feelings and what was happening to me I knew that they must have just returned me. I had no memory of the abduction, yet I knew it had happened. I closed my eyes again and began to meditate in an effort to free my mind. After several minutes of deep breathing and meditation, I was able to move again. I didn't tell Denise what had happened. I didn't know how I would explain it. I also didn't want to add any un-necessary stress on her. With her being pregnant, I knew that it wasn't the right time to reveal anything more to her about my abductions. Unfortunately, that time would reveal itself in the not too distant future.

Because of the unusual circumstances of Denise getting pregnant while on birth control pills; her OB/GYN had requested her to make frequent visits with him until he was assured that everything was normal with her pregnancy. Denise was in good health, and soon the doctor was pleased with everything; both mother and child were doing well. We were both relieved that no problems had been found. Everything was going along with the pregnancy as it should be. After a few more weeks, her gynecologist did an ultrasound. The ultrasound test also showed that the fetus was growing and progressing in a normal fashion. There was nothing in all of the exams and tests that indicated any sort of problem. Denise's doctor had told her to keep doing what she was doing and that he wouldn't need to see her now for a few weeks. That was all good news!

Then I began to experience the reoccurring nose bleeds again. One morning I woke up to again find small droplets of blood on my pillow. I couldn't hide this from Denise, so I just explained to her that I was having some sinus problems and must be blowing my nose too hard. I'm not sure if she believed me or not. A week or so later I woke up to find a substantial amount of blood stains littered about my pillow. The red blood drying against the pure white color of my pillow case created a very disturbing contrast. It was a symbolism of the truth; a glimpse of the consequences of a multi-dimensional reality crossing into my everyday reality. I stood and stared at it. I knew it was them. "Why are they coming for me so much?" I asked myself being careful not to show my dismay. "That can't be your sinus causing this Bret", Denise said. She continued, "You need to go to the doctor right away". "Calm down, calm down, I'm OK. Look, if it happens again I promise you that I will go to the doctor", I replied. "You promise?", She asked. "I promise. One more time and I'll go for sure" I said. That seemed to satisfy her for the time being. She seemed suspicious though, and I wondered if she knew that it was the Greys causing my nosebleeds from their procedures being done on me. If she did, she kept it to herself and never mentioned it. I was happy that she did. And then the unthinkable happened.

A few nights later while Denise and I were both sleeping soundly we were suddenly awakened by a loud bang in our bedroom. I quickly raised my head up to see what had caused the noise. As I did, I found that I was unable to move any other part of my body. There was a very bright light coming through the back window of the bedroom that lit the room up and there they were. Standing in our bedroom were five extraterrestrial beings! Small, thin, large heads, dressed in matching dark tight uniforms. It was the Greys. I was horrified! Maybe it was from fear or maybe it was the Greys using their mind control, but I couldn't get any sound to come out of my mouth. I looked over at Denise and saw that she was also awake. She too must have been rendered immobile. She wasn't moving or speaking either. She was just laying there with her eyes wide open and a look of sheer terror on her face. The aliens were all standing still with no movement what so ever. They stood there just staring at us with those big black eyes for what felt like an eternity. I don't think that they expected us to wake up when we did. From what I have observed during my abductions I have concluded that everything the small Greys do is based purely on logic. When something illogical happens it seems that it confuses the small ones, and they become unsure of how to react.

I remember that two of the aliens were standing along the side of the bed where Denise was at. There was a Grey at the foot of the bed in front of me and one standing beside it toward my side of the bed. One of the aliens had stayed in the back of the bedroom close to the area that opened up into the master closet and bath. I have no other memories of the aliens in our bedroom that night. It felt like everything went black about that time. The next thing I remember is opening my eyes and seeing a bright light. I was laying nude on some kind of hard surface table or bed that was just barely big enough to fit my body. I was completely surrounded my Greys. I didn't see any kind of medical equipment or exam devices around me this time. Just Greys, all standing very close around me on all sides. I knew that this time something different was going on or maybe had already gone on without me remembering it. I was scared! There was no way to know for sure what was happening or what was about to happen. I knew that there must be a reason for them to be surrounding me like they were. It was unusual for them to do that in the manner that they were.

I was still unable to move any other part of my body except my head. The Grey closest to my head leans over me; his face is within a foot of my face. I didn't want to look at him. I want to close my eyes, so I don't have to look at him, but I am unable to. He was forcing me to look at him; I couldn't resist his command. I was forced to look into those deep large black eyes of this insect looking creature. He begins to communicate telepathically with me. They usually would try to calm me down when doing this but this time they weren't. He told me that there was something he wanted me to see. The alien next to him must have known what he said to me. Right after he told me that there was something that he wanted me to see, the Grey standing on his right side next to him changed positions and moved around to the top of my head. I was getting very, very nervous. I hated it; the feeling of helplessness, the not knowing, and the apprehension of what was coming next. You never knew with these heartless bastards what they were going to do with you. I still don't!

When the Grey moved to the area at the top of my head, I turned my head to the right to see what else was in the in the room I was in. When I did, I was shocked to see Denise lying on another platform table about 15 feet away from me. She was also nude. There were several aliens around the platform she was on but not by her left side. They had purposely left me an open view to her. They had her legs up and spread very much like a typical gynecological exam that is done here. I was furious at what was happening! Denise started to scream. I want to scream too, but I still couldn't. It was obvious that they let her cries be heard so that that I could hear them. "Please stop! Please don't hurt my baby", Denise begged the creatures. I couldn't bear to watch what they were doing to her, so I turned my head away. I could hear her crying and pleading with these extraterrestrial savages. I knew that I could do absolutely nothing to stop them; I felt helpless, useless, and weak. I felt them commanding me to watch what was happening with Denise. I fought their desire with all the will power I could muster and maybe for a few brief seconds it was working. Then the one by the top of my head places his scrawny, clammy hand over the top of my forehead and turns my head back towards Denise. It was hopeless, and I knew it. I heard Denise again. "No! No! It's my baby! Please don't take my baby!" She begged. It was all more than I could handle. I began to play mind games with myself. I told myself that this wasn't real; that I was just having a very bad dream.

I tried to convince myself that all I needed to do was wake up, and everything would be alright. But this nightmare was real. I was living it and deep down I knew it was real. I had never before felt the kind of barbaric rage that I felt at that time. Suddenly I was able to speak and I started screaming at these insidious pieces of shit with all my might. "You Bastards! I'm going to kill you! I promise I will kill all of you little mother fuckers", I adamantly expressed! I meant every word of it too. My anger and rage was so intense that had I been able to, I know that I certainly would have carried out my promise and taken out as many of them as I possibly could have. Looking back now, I'm sure that they found it all very amusing. I was stupid. I had let them win. They wanted me to be upset. The Greys are intensely interested in our human emotions as I have stated in previous chapters of this book. Having experienced their mind experiments before, I soon came to my senses and realized what they were doing. I knew that they wanted me to observe the procedure they were doing to Denise so that they could monitor my emotional response to it. I also knew from past experiences that the only power I had in these kinds of situations was to do my best to show no emotion at all, and that is exactly what I did. I quit screaming and cursing at them. I quit looking at Denise and instead began to focus my attention on the lights of the equipment on the wall beside her. I did my best to block out what was happening to Denise. It wasn't easy. On the inside, I felt my heart was being ripped out, on the outside I remained stoic. I went into a zone and intensely concentrated on nothing but the lights of the equipment. It must have worked. That was the last thing that I remember from being on board their craft that night.

A beautiful, bright ray of sunlight was shooting through the bedroom curtains when I woke up the next morning filling the quiet room with an enhanced sense of calm. My body felt drained. I rose up and sat on the edge of the bed trying to clear my head. I noticed that I was not on my side of the bed. I leaned over and shook Denise.

"Wake up", I told her. I continued, "Look where you are at. You're on my side of the bed, and I was on your side when I woke up". "Do you have any idea how we got switched?" I asked. Before she could answer me, I noticed that the old typewriter that had been sitting on a small table near the bed had been knocked over. Then I remembered the loud bang we had heard. "Look, the typewriter fell off the table. I wonder how that happened", I said to Denise. It was then that I started to remember the Greys being in our bedroom after we heard the typewriter crashing to the floor. It was the aliens that had accidentally knocked over the old typewriter. It was right by where one of them had been standing. I was about to ask Denise if she remembered anything about what had happened, but before I could ask Denise noticed blood on the bed. She got up and went straight to the bathroom. Then I heard her yell to me, "Oh my God! I'm bleeding! Call the doctor now"! I quickly jumped up and got dressed. Denise yelled again from the bathroom, "something's wrong. Something's wrong with the baby"! I called the doctor and explained what was going on. The nurse got the doctor on the phone, and he said for us to come in immediately. We rushed as quickly as we could go to the doctor's office; which took about 15 or 20 minutes. Denise was examined, and an x-ray was taken. The doctor came back into our room with a distraught look on his face. "There is no baby", he bluntly said. "You had a miscarriage", he explained. He asked Denise if she saw any tissue come out of her and she replied that she had not. There was only blood, no tissue at all. "You must be mistaken", the doctor said. He continued, "You were four months into the term of carrying this child. There would have been tissue". Denise assured him that there was no tissue that came out so he insisted that Denise be checked into the hospital for a procedure called a D&C to clean out her womb of the remaining fetus tissue.

I waited patiently in the hospital waiting room while Denise's procedure was being done. My head was spinning from all that had transpired in the last several hours. I kept remembering the horror of the night before. I couldn't shake it. It felt to me as if the aliens wanted us to remember it. I knew that they had taken the fetus. I saw them do it! Both my Mother and Denise's Mother had come to the hospital for support. Even though I appreciated them coming, I wasn't saying much to either of them. I was drained and I knew that this event would be more emotional pain to carry with no way to release it and this time I wasn't alone. I blamed myself. If Denise had never met me, she would have never had to endure such an insufferable nightmare.

I looked up and saw the doctor coming towards me. As we all got up to greet him, he started shaking his head. I was worried. "Is Denise OK"? I asked. "She's fine, but this was the strangest thing I've ever seen. There was nothing in Denise's womb; no remaining tissue at all. Her womb was already cleaned. It was like the fetus just disappeared. I just saw her a few days ago and she had a perfectly normal pregnancy and now it's as if she had never been pregnant at all and we both know that certainly was not the case", the doctor replied. After the doctor walked away I looked at my Mother and said, "they took it". "Who took it?" She replied. "The Greys", I simply stated and said no more. I would later tell her what had happened but right then I didn't have the strength to talk about it. I just didn't have it in me. I didn't even want to think about.

Later that evening Denise was released from the hospital. I felt numb. I didn't know whether to scream or cry. I was exhausted both physically and mentally. I had nothing left. I didn't know what to say and I don't think that Denise did either. Maybe it was better that way. Maybe the silence somehow helped the healing process to begin. We both needed rest. The ride home from the hospital was somber and silent. I wasn't sure how much that Denise remembered and I didn't want to bring it up and cause her more emotional trauma so I kept quiet and waited. Several days would go by before Denise said anything and we were able to talk about what had happened that night to us and to the baby. To my dismay, Denise also remembered it all. The Greys hadn't blocked or erased the memory of the event from either of us. There was nothing left to say or do now. Another life had been changed forever. The baby takers had come to visit.

# Chapter 8

# Children of the Greys

There are civilizations on earth whose people claim to be descendants of those who came from the stars. Native American tribes such as the Cherokee and the Hopi know these beings as the Star People. The Hopi culture was derived by beings they call Kachinas. They believe the Kachinas were from other planets. Many tribes such as the Cherokee believe their ancestors originated in the Pleiades constellation. Other North American Native tribes such as the Cree and the Dakota all have similar beliefs. In her book, In Search Of Shambhala, Mary Sutherland writes:

*Native Americans believed in constellations in many cases they believed in the same formations for stars that we do. Their constellations seemed to be marked by the same knowledge that western civilizations on the other part of the globe was aware of. They call them by different names but the star arrangements were very similar.*

*They believed in maps that have been drawn. That they existed at the center of the earth or Turtle Island. (To the Anishinabe, North America is Turtle Island.) That beyond them was the sky and that beyond the sky were dimensional portals or sky holes as they called them. Beyond the dimensional portals was an area that they call the Ocean of Pitch, were the boundaries of the universe and that set along the rim at the boundaries of the universe were 4 different extraterrestrial groups.*

*They believed in Achivas (kivas) the sacred ceremonial places to honor the earth. These are the places that Shaman would go into the earth to do their most sacred work. The reason that Achivas are built into the earth for sacred work is because according to legend, at the destruction at each of the ages of mankind the people that were pure of heart went down into the buxom of the earth and there remained protected. According to them they dwelt in the center of the earth with a group of beings that they call the Ant People.*

*Drawing of the Ant People are remarkably similar to the Grey aliens of today-large heads-little stocky bodies- long spindly fingers-in some cases 4, 5, or 6 digits. Some of these drawings have the indication of telepathic waves coming from the beings' head themselves....*

*Early Dakota stories speak of the Tiyami home of the ancestors as being the Pleiades. Astronomy tells us that the Pleiades rise with the sun in May and that when you die your spirit returns south to the seven sisters.*

*The Hopis called the Pleiadians the Chuhukon, meaning those who cling together. They considered themselves direct descendants of the Pleiadians. The Navajos named the Plaeiades the Sparkling Suns of the Delyahey, the home of the Black God. The Iroquois pray to them for happiness.*

*The Cree claim to have come to earth from the stars in spirit form first and then became flesh and blood*

Throughout history, there are legends of beings from the sky either coming to earth to interact and teach humans or to breed/crossbreed. In many cases, these extra-terrestrial beings are attributed as being the fathers of mankind itself and were considered Gods by some ancient societies.

In 1850, excavator Austen Henry found ancient clay tablets in Iraq near the modern day city of Mosul. They turned out to be Sumerian text and were later deciphered by a linguistic scholar, Zechariah Sitchin. The ancient Sumerian text told about Gods they called the Annunaki, which translated from the Sumerian language, means, "those who from the sky (or stars) came". The ancient Sumerian text revealed that the Annunaki came from a planet in our solar system called "Nibiru". They came to earth to mine gold that was used on their planet. After a revolt of their people and needing more labor for their mining work, they decided to create workers for the mines. The text claimed that these aliens or, "Gods from the

stars" as they were called, mixed their DNA with one of the indigenous primates which quite possibly could have been Neanderthal
man since it has been proven by modern science that Neanderthal is
related to us. The Sumerian text goes on to claim that this genetic
manipulation by the Annunaki created us, Homo sapiens.

Although the history of the Sumerians found on these ancient
clay tablets may seem outlandish, there is actually some quite compelling evidence to back it up. Among numerous ancient civilizations throughout the world, there are many, many historical records,
artifacts, temples, and monuments as well as other archeological
evidence supporting the fact that the earth has been visited for mil-
lennium by extra-terrestrials. It is quite probable that these extra-
terrestrials beings have had a hand in shaping the evolution of
mankind and possibly even creating homo-sapiens. Science can
still not explain the sudden jump in the human evolutionary process
that occurred some 200,000 years ago, i.e. the missing link. Was it
alien intervention; the Annunaki, perhaps?

There are some researchers in the UFO field who don't believe
that these beings who are visiting us are actually extra-terrestrial
but instead are beings from other dimensions and not other planets
in outer space per se. In his book, Dimensions: A Casebook of Alien
Contact, the famed Ufologist, Jacques Vallee, speculated on this
conclusion:

*Or should we hypothesize that an advanced race somewhere in
the universe and sometime in the future has been showing us three-
dimensional space operas for the last two thousand years, in an
attempt to guide our civilization? If so, do they deserve our con-
gratulations? ... Are we dealing instead with a parallel universe,
another dimension, where there are human races living, and where
we may go at our expense, never to return to the present? Are these
races only semi human, so that in order to maintain contact with
us, they need cross-breeding with men and women of our planet?
Is this the origin of the many tales and legends where genetics
plays a great role: the symbolism of the Virgin in occultism and
religion, the fairy tales involving human midwives and change-
lings, the sexual overtones of the flying saucer reports, the biblical
stories of intermarriage between the Lord's angels and terrestrial
women, whose offspring were giants? From that mysterious*

*universe are higher beings projecting objects that can materialize and dematerialize at will?*

Although I don't adhere to Vallee's theories presented here, I do agree that there is a definite inter-dimensional aspect and the manipulation of them involved in the alien abduction events. I do find it very interesting that he entertains the thought of cross breeding by the semi human beings he speculates on as well as the role that this cross breeding has possibly played throughout mankind's existence in the multitude of historic tales, legends and cultural stories. Do I believe that aliens are responsible for all of these supernatural events recorded and/or passed down through the ages? No, of course not, and I am not saying that the inter-dimensional beings that Vallee believes responsible aren't responsible for some of the experiences that have happened and continue to happen. Quite possibly it could be both alien life forms and inter-dimensional beings either together or separately responsible. The important thing to acknowledge and recognize is, that is has happened and continues to happen. To ignore the overwhelming evidence of the alien abduction and or contactee phenomena is to ignore reality itself.

Given this long history of alien interest and interaction with the human race, it is not surprising that they are still here doing the same. Maybe it has not been the same alien species as in our past as it is now. Perhaps those species from man's ancient history has come, accomplished their mission for visiting earth, and left, never to return. Maybe different species of aliens have different reasons for their actions. I learned from firsthand experience the reason for the Greys sexual and reproductive procedures that had been done to me and now also to Denise.

The incident with Denise having the fetus removed by the Greys had severely damaged my psyche. I had always felt like nothing more than a laboratory specimen to them and now that feeling had been immensely intensified. I no longer felt the desire to resist my alien captors. They had won. They had broken me. From that point on, I would reciprocate their wishes. I had relinquished my will to fight and had accepted it as my fate. In some ways, it made it all easier. On subsequent abductions, they seemed to notice the change. I assumed that they read every thought not only in my mind at that time but other memories as well. Oddly enough, this change in me appeared to bother them. The routine changed. They weren't doing any of the mind experiments in the room where they would observe my emotional responses to my reality being altered by them. They actually seemed less obtrusive. They began to take me to areas I had never been to before. I co-operated on my own free will. I saw no use in resisting so where ever they asked me to go I would go on my own accord. They would not hold on to me as before. I would follow one or two of them, and there would be another one or two walking behind me. At times, there would only be one of them walking beside me. I just went where they led me; did what they asked me to do.

As time passed, something deep inside kept gnawing at me. I had come to understand why they did many of the things that they did and yet I kept wondering why they had taken the fetus from Denise and what they had done with it. They had taken sperm from me before. I'm sure they have done this numerous times throughout my life and that I don't recall all of them. Maybe due to the intrusive nature of the procedure my subconscious has protected me by not letting everything come to the surface. Even so, I know that they had my sperm. It was what they did with it that I didn't know. The thought that had haunted me for a very long time was about the fetus. I decided that I would ask them if I ever got the chance. I had no idea how they would respond to such an inquiry or if they would use that question against me in another one of their altered reality mind games they were so fond of. There had been times before when the tall one had answered my questions. Maybe he would answer this one without recourse. I wasn't sure what would happen, but I was sure that no matter what the consequences were, I was going to ask.

For a while there seemed to be a decrease in my unwanted visitors coming to get me or at least I don't have any memories of it if they did. It even got to the point that I began to believe that they were finished with me. Maybe they had gotten all they wanted from me. Maybe I was no longer of use to them. I had never gotten to ask them the important question about the fate of the fetus taken from Denise, but if it meant never having to experience another abduction again then I knew I could learn to live with it. I was foolish to believe in such a whimsical notion.

My hope of such freedom was shattered when I found myself once again opening my eyes to several Greys surrounding me on the intake table. It was an all too familiar feeling. After the examination was complete, I asked one of them if they would allow me to get up. He didn't answer, but I could feel my body becoming relaxed. I slightly moved my leg. I knew that I was no longer in a paralyzed state. The other Greys in the room stepped back as if they were being cautious. I don't believe that they were in fear of me since they easily could control my thoughts and through that, my actions, unless of course I was able to catch them off guard which is why they must have moved back.

I was standing naked by the platform I had been placed on. One of the smaller Greys was still standing close by me; he was the one I had spoken to and had asked if I could get up. I turned to him and said out loud, "I have a question for you". There was no response. He never moved nor did he in any way acknowledge I had spoken to him. I wasn't sure what to do, so I asked again. This time I just thought it. It didn't matter. The response was the same. I knew that the small ones could communicate because they had transmitted thought to me before. "Why isn't he responding?" I wondered. I took a couple of steps forward away from the examining table. All the aliens were standing very still and observing my every move. I tried a different approach. "May I speak to your leader, the tall one?" I asked. He must have been near. Perhaps he was watching all of this and knew, or maybe the small Grey telepathically contacted him because within a matter of seconds the "tall one" showed up. As I have previously said in this book, the tall one has always made an attempt to present himself to me as a friend. It's been that way from the very beginning. Through it all, I think he has always wanted me to trust him and not fear him. He has been the most civil to me even though he may well have been the guiding force behind all the despicable things these creatures have done to me over the years.

Suddenly I hear him in my head. "What is the question you ask of me?" He asked me. This was it. This was my one chance and maybe the only chance I was ever going to have to find out what had happened to the fetus. I never saw the tall one that night the nefarious act was done still I'm sure that he knew about it. "My baby, where is the baby you took from Denise?" I boldly asked. "Come with me. I will show you", he replied. I was quite surprised by his immediate response and also very suspicious. I felt a bit apprehensive, but I was willing to take the chance on whatever was going to happen next.

The tall alien led me down a narrow hall. I calmly walked along beside him to his right side. We hadn't gone far when we turned left into an open entrance. The lighting radically changed as we entered the room. The hallway was brightly lit; this room was not. I had never seen a room this dark before anywhere on their craft. The entire ambiance of this area was completely different from anywhere else on their ship that I had been taken to before if that is indeed what I was on. I stopped walking as I entered. The tall Grey stopped a step or two ahead of me when he saw that I had stopped walking. I still saw no other Greys which was unusual. The tall Grey turned his shoulder around toward me. Then he extended his left arm out toward the dim multi colored, lit area of the room. "Here is the answer you seek", he said to me telepathically. I slowly stepped forward walking past the tall Grey. He stood and watched me as I moved forward. I was in what I can only describe as some sort of elaborate laboratory. There were rows of round clear vials each about two feet tall. There were tubes hooked up to them which were filled with a liquid substance. I couldn't believe what I was seeing as I stood in front of one of the vials. Inside the vial was a small fetus! I quickly stepped back in shock. I looked down the row of clear vials and could see that all of the ones within my sight also contained fetuses. I wish now that I would have taken a closer look to see if they were human or hybrid fetuses, but I didn't. I can only speculate at this point. Perhaps there were both human and hybrid fetuses in that room. The clear vials seemed to me to be serving as a womb of sorts with computer monitoring and appeared to be keeping the fetuses alive. It was technology beyond anything I understood.

I walked out of the room, and the tall Grey followed me. I was trying not to show any emotion. I stood in the hall outside the entrance to the laboratory room. I turned toward the alien and asked, "Is that real? Did you create that in my mind or is that real"? Suddenly he began to fill my mind with more answers than I had asked for. He told me that it was very real. He said that they needed my baby and other human fetuses. He said they needed human sperm and eggs. He went on and blatantly stated that they were creating a new species; a hybrid mix of us and them. I wanted to know why, but that was all I received. This was one of the few times that I ever felt empathy for these frail insect looking creatures. I sensed desperation in him. I looked at him and thanked him. He remained motionless and said nothing more. It was all starting to make perfect sense now. They saw in our human species what they lacked in themselves. I've always felt that they were no longer able to reproduce or at least reproduce in a physical matter as we do. They admire the physical specimen that humans are. They are devoid of emotion and crave that simple aspect of the human psyche. They are fascinated by human sexuality, the physical act of sex and the emotions attached to it. I was coming to a clear understanding as to why they had done the procedures and put me through the experiences that they had. It made it all easier on me, and perhaps that is exactly what the intention of the tall Grey was. Why, after all those years of them taking me, all the procedures done on me, and all of the experiments, did he finally reveal this shocking revelation to me? That is an answer I still don't know and maybe never will know, although I will always be thankful that he did.

Are humans really all that different? We have done hideous experiments on untold thousands of animals for our own gain and well being. We've even done it to humans. If we were in their position, I am positive that we too would do whatever it took to save our species, and that is exactly what I feel is the scenario with the Greys. I have always been against animal testing for any reason. I know that there are many that would disagree with that, but I look at it from a different perspective than most. I've been the one who is getting tested on, felt the pain both mental and physical of procedures that you don't want done on you but have no way to stop. I understand the fear that goes through these poor defenseless animals' minds as we commit these cruel heartless acts on them. I don't believe that humans care anymore than the Greys do. It's all a means to an end.

The experience of seeing the fetuses in the vials was not the end of my encounters with the hybrid babies of the Greys. It was only the beginning. About 2 to 3 years after the incident of the aliens taking the fetus from Denise, I experienced a most unusual event during an abduction. I have no memories of anything else that happened during this particular abduction except being a participant in this one profound experience. I was led by two small Greys to a large open room. It was dark with only dim lighting that was coming from a source that I couldn't see. I could tell that the room was oval shaped with what appeared to be a rounded ceiling. I was clothed in some tight fitting garment. They took me to a spot that was at the edge of what looked like the floor turning into a ramp as it began to tilt down. There was a long white wall about 3 feet high to my right that had a white railing on top of it. It led down the ramp, but it was too dark to see exactly where it led to. One of my two alien escorts telepathically told me to stay then both the small Greys turned around and left. I didn't question them. I just obeyed even though I was alarmed by all the darkness and concerned about what was in store for me next. I had never been to this area before nor had I ever been subjected to the almost complete darkness of this room in any area of their craft before. I cannot say with certainty that I was in a craft. I could have been in some kind of alien facility. I have no way of knowing for sure. I only knew that I did not recognize the location that I had been taken be to.

I didn't have to wait long to find out why I had been taken to this room. Within a minute of the small Greys leaving, I saw a bright light suddenly appear about 75 feet away coming from an opening down the ramp in the direction I was facing. The light was too bright to see inside the opening and yet oddly enough it was not hurting my eyes to look into the light. I noticed that even though the opening was large, and the light coming from the room was extremely bright that the light stopped at the opening and did not filter into the larger room that I was in. The light sources of these alien crafts or facilities sometimes look as if there is some kind of invisible curtain that is stopping the light source from defusing light as we understand the properties of it will do.

From out of the light I saw a small frail figure walking my way. As the figure approached me and passed through the light source some of the light began to filter into the room I was in which continued to remain dimly lit although I now could see more clearly than I was able to before. As the figure got closer, I could see that it was a hybrid. It was taller than the small Greys but not as tall as the tall leader that I had previously encountered. The hybrid had whitish blonde shoulder length hair that was thin and wispy. Because of this, I assumed the figure was a female. She wore a thin white loose fitting garment that was similar to a nightgown and much like the one I had seen on the other female hybrid I had met. As she got closer, I noticed that she was carrying a small child hybrid. She stopped when she got to the level area of the floor and put the child down. The child was big enough and strong enough to be able to stand on its own. It too appeared to be female. The hybrid child had the same color of whitish blonde hair that the older hybrid did except it didn't quite reach her shoulders. She was dressed in the same type of clothing that the older hybrid was wearing. We all were standing about six feet apart. I wasn't sure what to say or do. I didn't know what to expect next, so I just stood silently looking at both of the hybrids.

Finally, the older hybrid spoke to me telepathically just like the Greys. "She is yours", she said, referring to the small child hybrid. I shook my head in disagreement. Here we go again I thought, more mind games to mess with my emotions. "I don't believe you", I replied. She walked the hybrid child over next to me. "I would like for you to hold her, speak to her", the older hybrid said. I replied rather emphatically, "No! I don't want to." My answer didn't stop her from her mission. She then grabbed my forearm to place my hand in the hybrid child's hand as she raised the hand of the child to meet mine. I don't know why but I did not resist. The little hybrid child showed no emotion at all. I knelt down on one knee and looked into the face of the little girl hybrid. Her eyes were bigger than human eyes but not as big as the eyes of the grey aliens. They weren't all black like the Greys' eyes either. Their color was more of a grey to light blue, and they were very human like in appearance. There was a certain softness to them. She looked up at me and didn't seem to be frightened by the obvious differences in our appearances as one would think might happen with a young child. It was almost as if she knew me or had seen me before. Maybe she had. Maybe we had met before, and I just didn't remember it.

Within seconds of touching this child and looking into her eyes, I felt an emotional attachment to her. I felt compelled to speak to her. "Hello, it's very nice to meet you", I said. She didn't reply and yet I still felt that she enjoyed me attempting to communicate with her. I continued, "Would you like to sit on my knee? ", I asked. Without waiting for a response from her I impulsively took her in my arms and sat her on my knee. She looked back at the older female hybrid when I did this and then back at me. I smiled at her hoping that she would understand that I meant her no harm. She was holding on to my arm and looking at me. She wasn't just looking in my eyes. She was looking at my entire body. She seemed to notice that I looked different than her. I remember continuing to try to talk with her. "I like your hair", I told her as I touched the side of her head and ran my fingers across her hair. "My name is Bret, what is your name?" I asked her. I don't know if she didn't know how to speak with me or was told not to but she would never respond verbally to anything I said to her. I sensed that she liked it though, and I could sense that she liked me.

The longer I was with this small hybrid child, the stronger my attachment to her became. I really wanted to know her name if she had one. I had never been told a name of any of the Greys during any of the many times I have been taken by them. Maybe they don't have a need for names in their structured environment or maybe they just never felt a need to tell me their names. I don't know; I was hoping that the hybrids might be different. I stood up still holding the child. "What is her name?" I asked the older hybrid. "It is now time for me to leave", she replied. She walked over to me and took the hybrid child from my arms. As she turned to walk back down the ramp toward the opening I once again asked, "Please, will you please tell me her name?" I had a burning desire to know her name. I wanted something to remember her by. The older female hybrid never answered. She kept walking into the bright light of the opening until I no longer could see them. Soon the opening closed, and I found myself once again the solemn darkness of the room I was in surrounded by silence. I felt confused by what had just happened. I can't explain it, but I also felt sadness. I wondered if I ever would see the little girl again. I couldn't understand why I suddenly felt such an emotional attachment to this hybrid child. I believe now that perhaps the older hybrid was telling me the truth when she told that the child was mine. Was the child a result of cross hybridization from the fetus they had taken from Denise? Or was my sperm used to create her? I will probably never know for sure. I have always hoped that someday, on a subsequent abduction that I would meet this same hybrid girl again but so far that has never happened. I still hold on to that hope.

My last encounter with a humanoid looking baby was a stark contrast to meeting the little hybrid girl. This event happened in 2011 and also involved what I perceived as humans working in conjunction with the alien Greys. Instead of opening my eyes to find myself in the "intake" area, as I had many times before during these abductions, I ended up on a table in a very large room. The lighting was different this time. It had a more washed out sterile brightness to it than what I had noticed in other areas they had taken me to. The room was sparse. It also seemed that it was too large for what it was being used for. This time a tall Grey was there beside the table I was on. It was not the tall Grey I had previously been with. Although, much like the other tall Grey, he seemed to be more cordial to me. He asked me to get up off the table. Much to my surprise I found that I was able to move easily as I did what he had asked me to do. There were other Greys in the room who for some reason didn't appear that interested in me. "Come with me", the tall Grey ordered as he started walking toward an opening. I walked beside him through the opening that led out into a very wide hallway that was also brightly lit. I was still nude. This was sometimes the case when they took me somewhere. I felt much more comfortable and at ease than I normally did. There is something about the tall Grey leaders that gives me this feeling. It has always been that way since the very beginning of these experiences.

While the tall Grey and I were walking down the hallway, I began to suspect that they were going to do another sexual procedure of some kind on me. There was no need to ask him where we were going or what they were going to do. Even if he decided to tell me I knew it would make no difference. I knew that I was helpless in stopping it so why bother asking. I saw several other smaller Greys moving about the hallway as if actively engaged in their work. None of them acknowledged my presence. Whatever it was that they were doing didn't seem to have anything to do with me. I thought that this was very strange. Everything in this place I was in was so orderly and organized. I felt like that I was not on a craft but in some kind of facility somewhere. It was all very different than before.

I was looking down this large hall to try and see where we were going to when I saw him. A human male! I was very surprised to see this man for several reasons. The most important of which was that he was freely walking about with no alien escorts of any kind. I couldn't believe it! "Maybe he is under mind control", I thought to myself. I was careful to monitor my thoughts since I knew that they could read my mind. I believed this man to be human although I had no way to know for sure. He was an average size man in both height and weight. He had short dark hair and was dressed in a tight fitting black outfit that looked like a uniform of some sort. It was very much like the kind of clothing that I had sometimes been put in during an abduction. He was carrying what I thought was a baby that was wrapped in a small white blanket. I couldn't tell for sure what the object was that the man was carrying since it was completely wrapped up but from the size of the object and the way that he was carrying it I assumed it must be a baby. Then I became even more puzzled. What was this man doing walking down the hall with a baby and why? The tall Grey stopped as the man approached us. The tall Grey was to my right and three or four feet ahead of me. The man walked past the tall Grey and stopped directly in front of me. "Who are you?" I asked him. "It doesn't matter who I am", he replied. That was not the answer I wanted or expected. So I asked, "What are you doing here? Why are you here?" He opened up the white blanket wrapped around the object he was holding. "To show you this", he answered.

It was a baby, and it was alive. It did not look anything like the little hybrid girl that they had brought to me years earlier. This poor baby was hideous looking! It looked to be very young. Possibly only a couple of months hold by human comparison. This sad little thing was severely deformed, especially the head and facial features. The man had turned the baby around to face me. He was holding it at about his mid torso. From what I could tell the baby was not wearing anything. The baby looked very human like except for the head and face. It had a body and skin like ours but looked nothing like a human from the neck up. I looked at the tall Grey and then back to the man holding the baby. I was determined not to react in any way.

I stood there looking at the man and the baby without saying a word. I held steadfast in my determination not to show any emotion. The man had a look of frustration on his face, but he never spoke either. He looked over at the tall Grey. I don't think he knew what he was supposed to do next. There was no verbal exchange between him and the tall Grey that I heard audibly. I assume the tall Grey must have communicated with him because as soon as the man did that he turned his head back to the baby, covered it up in the blanket again and walked away in the opposite direction of me. I knew that they were once again testing me, monitoring my emotional reaction but this time they failed. I have become very adept in shutting down my emotions, and this time was no exception.

My mind has gotten much stronger since the experiments they performed on me in those early years. It felt good! It was another small but significant win for me in my war of empowerment with these alien beings. I never found out who the human male was or what he was doing there. It was obvious that he was working with the Greys. I'm sure that he wasn't alone. There had to have been other humans there with him. I've often pondered the notion that this alien human interchange has been going on for a very long time. Was the deformed baby the man in the black uniform was holding a result of some failed cloning or hybrid experiment? Or was it an alien whose appearance was natural to their species but perceived as appalling to mine? I don't know the answers to these questions. I can only speculate on them and even why they showed it to me in the first place. If my lack of response upon viewing the grotesque baby bothered the tall Grey, he certainly didn't show it. He nonchalantly turned around and continued walking down the hallway without saying anything to me or even indicting for me to come with him. I went along with him anyway. The last thing I remember is being led to another large room. What happened there is locked away somewhere deep within the recesses of my subconscious, and perhaps it is best that is where it remains.

# Chapter 9

# The Never Ending, Never Ending Story

Tat, tat, tat, tat. Tat, tat, tat, tat. I was awakened by the sound of something or someone striking the side of my mattress. I was lying on my left side facing the master bedroom closet and a wall. I could feel the bed vibrate from the quick succession of hits that were coming from the edge of the bed down around my knees. I thought it was a ghost since my wife Gina and I have had these kinds of paranormal occurrences happen to us before, so I didn't immediately open my eyes. I wanted to see what it would do next in order to get my attention. I waited; nothing else happened, so I assumed that it must have given up and left. I slowly opened my eyes without moving my head so as not to make it disappear just in case it was still there. Instantly I felt a rush of adrenalin shoot through my veins! Standing right next to me beside my bed were three Greys! They were all lined up side by side down the edge of the mattress. I immediately noticed something very peculiar. There was an oval shape on the bedroom wall, that looked like what I can best describe as a mirage in the desert with the wavy lines, that I could see through. It looked like an opening that went into another room. There was another Grey standing far back inside this room. The opening had a white, misty substance around the edges of it that was about a 12 to 18 inches wide. The opening itself was close to 8 feet across in the widest section and almost 7 feet in height at its highest point.

The three Grey aliens started to reach for me. My first thought was to wake Gina so that possibly she could escape. Under no circumstances did I want them to take her too. I tried to turn around toward her to wake her, but I couldn't move. So I tried to call out to her. I opened my mouth to yell; nothing would come out no matter how hard I tried. I was so angry! I spoke to the aliens with my thoughts. "Please don't take her" I begged of them. "Please don't take her", I repeated. I was being lifted up by some kind of force. I knew that they were going to take me into the oval shape which I believe must have been some kind of dimensional portal. I tried to shout again, "No!" I could hear myself physically shouting it this time, but it was to no avail. When I started to shout out loud I was in the bedroom but before I finished that single word, I was gone. It happened that fast. I don't know if they took Gina that night. She has no memory of anything happening to her. In fact, when I told her the next morning what had happened she said that she had slept straight through the night without waking, which is very unusual for her to do. I don't know what they did to me during that particular abduction. I only remember screaming out and then in a flash I was in the room I had seen through the portal.

This event happened this year. The abductions keep happening. The Greys haven't lost their interest in me. To this day they keep coming for me. As time has passed, the abduction experiences have changed somewhat. At times, my anger towards the Greys returns. I feel that they know this. I've purposely attempted to send out telepathic messages to them and expressed my anger at them. I've told them how I won't let them take me anymore without fighting them with everything I have. I've called them names and threatened them.

I believe that the implants they have placed in me, enables them to read and monitor my every thought at will, so I'm sure that they have found my actions to be very entertaining. These brief episodes of lashing out angrily at the Greys don't last long. I always go back to giving in like I have for years. I suppose I threaten them more for my own healing than anything. It helps me to deal with it all. It gives me some sense of empowerment even if only for a few fleeting moments. It helps to release the anger that builds up from not being in control of what these insidious looking creatures do to me repeatedly. I have read articles that claimed that you could stop an alien abduction simply by rebuking them in the name of Jesus. I can't speak for others, but I can assure you that this simple technique does not stop the Grey aliens from taking this hapless victim. Perhaps the authors of these kinds of articles consider the aliens to be demonic and thus believe that one can banish them this way. I will not get into the religious connotations of either the paranormal or of the alien abduction phenomenon here. I will only reiterate that I don't believe it is possible to stop the particular alien species that have taken me my entire life in this manner, no matter how strong ones religious convictions might me. If it were that easy, I would have stopped them a long time ago.

Things have changed in recent years concerning my ability to block the Greys from suppressing so much of my memory of the abduction experiences. I am now able consciously to remember at least a part of most of every event. Another thing that has changed is the frequency of the abductions. Thankfully, they have slowed down. Perhaps I am still of use to them but not as much as when I was younger. Or perhaps they cannot control my emotions like they once could. I have worked hard on my mental capabilities. I also now practice Reiki, and I know just how strong my energy flow is. I get the sense that they are leery of me now so maybe they choose not to come as often. This is pure speculation on my part as there is no way for me to really understand the rationale behind why they don't come for me as often as they once did. I only know that I am glad that they don't.

I have been meeting an unusual amount of other alien abductees the past couple of years. Whether this is by coincidence or by fate is hard to say. I have always felt like a wayward ship lost at sea with no one to share these traumatic events with. It's loneliness that is difficult to describe. I live a double life as I try to maintain some sense of normalcy; while all these things are being done to me by beings that I don't fully understand much less expect anyone else to. It has been quite liberating being able to meet and speak with others who can understand and relate to me in a way than only those of us who have experienced these traumatic events can. Sometimes these people have a certain familiarity about them. Like we have seen each other before and maybe in some cases we have seen each other during an abduction. Or maybe, it's just that bond that all abductees have. We don't have to speak of it. It is just there naturally. It is not often that I come across someone who I believe has been abducted but I am often able to know intuitively if someone has experienced these alien abductions. It's something that has developed over the years. Sometimes I will bring it up to them and sometimes I won't. If I don't think that they remember, then I will usually let it be as I believe that there are things that are better off left buried. Let them discover their own truths in their own time.

One abductee I met recently was a woman who I met through Sandy Nichols, who I mentioned earlier. Sandy is a mutual friend of hers and mine. To protect her privacy, I will reference her as Susan and not use her real name here. In the spring of 2010, I was giving a presentation to a paranormal Meet Up group on Electronic Voice Phenomenon, or EVP. These are recordings of spirit communication obtained during a paranormal investigation. Gina and I are paranormal investigators and work under the name of Halo Paranormal. We are known for capturing large numbers of EVP's and will sometimes do presentations on the subject. During my presentation, I noticed Susan sitting in the back of the room. I didn't know who she was at the time, but I got that feeling I get when I am around another abductee. After the presentation was over, Gina and I were approached by several people asking us questions about the paranormal and telling us of their own ghost experiences. We always try to oblige and help in any way we can so we spent quite a bit of time that night engaging in conversation with those that had come up to us to ask questions and meet us. Due to so many people speaking with us, we never got to meet Susan that night.

A few days later, Sandy asked us over to his house and said that he was inviting a quest who was very interested in our paranormal work and wanted to meet us. Much to our surprise, it was Susan. We had an enjoyable evening discussing the paranormal and doing some paranormal experiments. Sometime during the course of the conversation that night the subject of alien abductions got brought up. I confessed that I had been having abduction experiences since I was five years old. Sandy already knew this about me and had become a confidant as we shared our various experiences and the trauma they inflicted upon us. Susan must have felt comfortable with us because she soon confirmed my intuitions; she confessed that she too had been an experiencer.

Susan explained that she felt that her experiences were MILABS, which are joint military and alien abductions. She only remembered bits and pieces of these abductions but enough to know that they had taken place. Like me, and I'm sure many others, she had trusted very few people with these revealing and personal revelations. At that time, I had no memories of ever seeing any human, military personnel present during an abduction. After meeting Susan, that would change. It was only a couple of months after meeting Susan when I had the experience of seeing the human in the black uniform that was carrying the deformed looking baby that was showed to me. It is certainly within the realm of possibilities that he was military. Then in 2012 it happened again during an abduction.

I woke up in a place that I had never seen before. It was dimly lit. The soft glow of the light seemed to be coming from a line of equipment on a wall by the foot of the platform I was laying on. The observation table I was placed on felt cold on my naked body. It was the usual platform like bed with rounded edges. As was usually the case, I couldn't move anything but my head. There was a white counter type piece of furniture to my left that reminded me of what you see in a doctor's office. Beyond that, I could see a light coming through from an open doorway that was on the wall behind my head. I turned my head to the right. I could see that there was another person laying on a second silver colored platform surrounded by Greys. I tried to look between the aliens around the platform to get a better view of the person laying on it. I couldn't see the person well enough to tell if they were male or female although I could see that the person also that appeared to be nude. I didn't hear any sound coming from the person lying on the platform which got me to wondering what the aliens were doing to them. I didn't know if they were even alive.

My heart began to pound furiously as I thought about what the aliens might have planned to do to me this time. So many questions were racing through my mind. Why was it so dark in the place they had taken me? It's usually very bright on their craft. I wondered where I was. I noticed that even the equipment didn't look the same as what I had seen before when they had taken me. The white counter to my left was not the shape and size of other furniture I had witnessed at any previous alien locations. In fact, it looked very normal to me, very much like our earth made furniture. I felt confused and nervous. I could feel the adrenalin racing through my veins. I wanted out of this situation. I wanted out now!

I wanted answers, but the creatures weren't paying any attention to me much less communicating anything to me. My nervousness grew to the point of agitation. I know how to speak to them, so I began to telepathically send my thoughts to the Greys. It worked; two of the Greys that were standing beside the other person a few feet away to my right walked over to me. They attempted to use their usual array of what had become to me by now "useless" calming phrases. "Calm down", one of them said telepathically and he placed his hand on the side of my head. He continued, "You know we won't hurt you." I had heard them say similar things to me so many times before that it was now condescending to me for them to speak to me like that. "Where am I?", I asked with a demanding tone. I continued, "What are you going to do to me?" The Greys kept true to their script and continued to repeat their statements to me in an attempt to ease my nervousness and agitation.

It was then that I heard the sound of footsteps coming from the doorway. I quickly turned my head back to the left in the direction towards the sound of the footsteps I heard. As I did, I saw two human men in tight fitting black uniforms enter. The uniforms the men were wearing were exactly like the one I had seen on the man who had showed the deformed baby to me in the hallway while I was walking with the tall Grey. These men looked very human to me.

They were escorting a short human female with dark hair. She was also naked. The men were on each side of her. They were each holding on to one of her arms as they guided her into the room where I was at. They began to walk towards me. They came out of the shadows of the darkness and stopped by the white counter. It was then as the trio entered under the dim lighting that I got a good look at them. As I did my eyes widen in shock. I couldn't believe it! I knew this woman. It was Susan! She had her eyes open, yet she appeared to be drugged or in a trancelike state. She didn't seem to recognize me or really be aware of anything going on in the room. I had seen other humans before during the sex experiments that also exhibited behavior similar to the way Susan was acting and responding to her surroundings.

I spoke to her, "Susan. It's me Bret". She didn't seem to hear me. She just stood there with this blank look on her face staring out across the room. Again I tried to speak to her, "are you OK?', I asked. Once again there was no reply or acknowledgement from her of my question. The men had let go of Susan's arms and were standing about a foot behind her. One of them commanded me in English to stop trying to talk to her. Interestingly enough, the Greys didn't seem to care that I was attempting to talk to her or that I recognized her. Neither the aliens nor the men in the black uniforms appeared to be surprised that I knew Susan. I suspect that whatever else happened that night had been planned long before they took both of us. I had noticed that Susan had something black about the size of a silver dollar in circumference stuck to the right side of her groin area. It looked like she had been tagged with something. Maybe I too had been tagged, but I couldn't see that part of my body. Was this black piece sticking on her side some kind of device that controlled her and made her act in the way she did? Was she drugged or was it mind control? Maybe it was something they used during whatever experiments or examinations they did to her or any of us other humans taken that night? I don't know. I don't remember anything else from that night. I don't have those answers. What I do know is I have now experienced two alien abductions where there were what I perceived as human military personnel, working in conjunction with the Grey aliens......

Gina and I ended up becoming good friends with Susan. We still keep in touch with her and visit when we can. I have revealed to her the details of what happened the night I saw her during that particular abduction. Although she doesn't have any conscious memories of it, she was not shocked by my revelation to her. She did say that she had recently noticed an increase in paranormal activity and unusual things happening to her that she cannot explain. These sorts of things happening to her throughout her life have not been uncommon; however, we both were intrigued by the fact that there had been this sudden increase which coincided with the timing of the mutual abduction we experienced together. I now wonder if my meeting Susan was not by chance but planned. Had the Greys brought us together for some unknown reason? Are there other experiencers out there that they have done the same thing to? With

Susan having a background of experiencing MILAB's, did this coincide with me now witnessing military type personnel working with the aliens? I now have more questions than answers.

I am left with the very real possibility that my own future personal abduction experiences may sometimes consist of involvement from these humans in the black uniforms. I have no other recourse but to question the likely malevolent motive of the humans involved with the aliens. I can understand the possible alien motives and the reasons behind them, but I don't understand what our own people and/or government would be using us for much less why they would do it in conjunction with the Greys. Still, I've seen them there working alongside of the aliens, and I'm not alone. Other experiencers have reported seeing humans working with the aliens during their own personal abductions. Personally, I don't remember humans conducting any procedures on me, but that doesn't mean that it hasn't happened; only that I don't remember it if it has.

If our government knows that the Greys are taking its citizens and doing nothing about it, then I can only assume that either they have made some kind of deal with them, perhaps a trade of sorts for technology. Maybe they had no choice knowing full well that they were up against a far superior weapon technology. Or perhaps our government knows that the Greys would not need any weapons to win a war with earthlings because the power of their minds are such that they could render us defenseless merely by thought alone. If there is a faction of our government that is also a part of these abductions and they are participating by choice and on their own accord, then that is not only tragic but very alarming for not only the victims like me but for us all.

The paranormal has been a part of my life since the Greys first took me as a young child. I began to have ghostly visitations soon after my first abduction which continue to this day. As I have stated before, I am firmly convinced that there is a direct connection between the two. Everything is energy, and I believe that somehow mine and other experiencers energy are altered by a dimensional shift that occurs in the way the aliens take and return their human subjects. I believe that the vibrational rate of an abductee's energy is increased by this. My research into the realm of spirits and ghosts has led me to believe that they exist in another dimension close to the dimension of the living and that they are once again in pure energy form once they cross over to that dimension. This energy form vibrates at a faster rate than that of the living in the dimension we exist in. Many times while recording EVPs (electronic voice phenomena), I have found that the EVPs are spoken at a much faster rate than the normal speed of human speech. Often, the EVPs will have to be slowed down in audio software in order to understand what the spirit speaking was saying. I attribute this differential in speech patterns, rates, and frequencies to the increased rate of the spirit energy and the dimensional shift that takes place when we die. I believe that a similar change takes place in the body energy of abductees, and when we are returned we carry over the increased energy vibration speed caused by crossing through dimensions.

It took me a long time to wrap my head around that concept but to me nothing else explains how the Greys are able to conduct the activity that they do and go virtually unseen. Other abductees have reported being taken through walls without any physical repercussions from it. Many witnesses of paranormal activity have reported seeing ghosts walk through walls as if the wall wasn't there. If one is in another dimension with different physical characteristics, then, in fact, the wall is not there. The Greys are indeed opening up portals and traveling between and through dimensions. Worm holes? Bending gravity? How they do it is beyond my comprehension or scientific knowledge, but I've experienced it. I've seen it. It's being done, and it's being done well.

It took me decades to accept and understand just why I attracted so many in the spirit world to me. Now I know that because of my many abductions my energy is more like theirs. I'm like a beacon to them. I've endured just about every kind of paranormal experience that there is; short of being possessed, which I believe, would never happen because my energy is much too strong for that and my belief system is not regimented to such. When I was a child, I was terrified by all the things I saw, felt and heard. When some paranormal event would happen, I would tell adults. Sometimes they would listen but then they would tell me that there were no such things as ghosts so it must have been something else that caused whatever it was that happened. Eventually, I learned to deal with it, and I gained strength and the courage to confront the spirits. As I grew older, I became less and less afraid of the spirit world and those who reside in it. I now embrace it.

Whether or not the Greys know it, but they have given me a gift. I am now happy to have this increased body energy. I know now that most of the time when a spirit speaks to me, moves something or appears to me that they aren't trying to scare me as most people would believe. They are seeking me out for help. They are lost, confused, even scared themselves. Gina and I capture large amounts of EVP's during paranormal investigations, and now I know why. We try and use what the spirits/ghosts tell us to help them. We pray for them when they ask us to. We explain to them what has happened to them. We try to comfort them and explain to them what we feel they should do in order to progress. We use our paranormal work and spirit communication efforts to help both the living and the dead. They still come to me just as they did when I was a child. They appear to Gina and me at night by our bed. They move things in our house. They open doors and turn lights off and on, bang on the walls and they speak to us. Anything to get our attention. It is a way of life for us. For decades, I've suffered at the hands of these strange looking alien beings. I've taken this particular attribute that was derived from my abductions and used it to make a positive difference in both the lives of the living and the dead. Gina has always had a shared interest in the paranormal and in UFO's and their inhabitants. She has readily accepted the same responsibility to the spirit world as I have. She has also been very understanding and supportive in dealing with both the trauma of my past abduction experiences and the ongoing current events. It is because of her and my good friend Sandy Nichols encouragement that I have come forward and revealed my alien encounters to the world.

Through our research into various methods of spirit communication, Gina and I discovered the process that was first used by Nikola Tesla that I previously mentioned. This process is ITC (Instrumental Trans Communication) which is any form of spirit communication through the means of electrical devices. We began to use the device commonly referred to as a "Ghost Box" or a "Spirit Box" on a regular basis and still do. When Tesla reported publicly that he heard voices coming through the radio frequencies there were no radio stations or any other possible cause for the voices other than the voices of the dead. The great inventor, Thomas Edison, also believed that speaking with spirits was possible using radio waves and frequencies. He was said to have been working on his own such device when he died which he had aptly named the "Telephone to the Dead".

Gina and I introduced the Spirit Box to two close friends of ours who are also contributors to this book, Brent Raynes and Sandy Nichols. We have all been using the Spirit Box for several years now and have achieved amazing results. On the night that we decided to try and contact the Greys while conducting a Spirit Box session at the home of Sandy Nichols, we received some very interesting replies; one of which was the "it was for life" reply we heard after I had asked about the scar on my back. When we first began the session that night nothing happened. The only thing we heard coming from the Spirit Box was static. This was unusual since we often hear replies from the spirits rather quickly. We kept repeating some of the questions and then we began to hear replies. Oddly enough, the replies that we were receiving sounded more like a computer generated voice than the spirit voices we were used to hearing and they seemed to be direct intelligent answers to our questions. I had asked about the scar on my back and had gotten an answer. So Sandy and I asked more questions pertaining to our abductions, and we continued to receive answers. We asked what alien race as we call them that were we speaking with. "Greys", was the reply. "What is it you need from us?", We asked. A voice replied, "Sperm". We then asked, "What do you use our sperm for?" A voice quickly answered, "Babies"! None of us present that night knew what to think about it. I don't think any of us really believed that we were communicating with the Greys, but we were all extremely perplexed as to how we were getting these answers that coincided with questions about our abductions.

About a week before we had conducted the Spirit Box session that night, I had been taken again. I only remembered a very short part of what had happened to me during that abduction still, I remembered it very clearly. I had seen a piece of equipment used on me by the Greys that I had never seen before. During this abduction, I was taken to a small room and placed on the same kind of examining table as I have previously described. This room was not brightly lit. In fact, it was dark and very dimly lit. There were six of the small Greys there, three on each side of me. The only light in the room seemed to be coming from the equipment on the wall to my right. I could move freely but for some reason felt no desire to. I felt very calm. Maybe they had done something to me before I was taken to that room that kept me calm. If so, I don't remember it, but for some reason I felt safe and not nervous about whatever procedure they were about to perform on me.

The alien on my right side who was the closest to my head leaned over me like they usually do. He was right in front of my face. His large eyes looking like endless pits of black oil were only inches from my own eyes. I wanted to look away but couldn't. "We are going to use a device on your body. You must close your eyes as we begin", he said to me. He leaned back up and stepped away from me. All the aliens on my right side moved toward the wall with the equipment. I watched as they pulled from the wall a large half-moon shaped object that was about 2 1/2 wide and 6 to 7 feet long. It was metallic on the top rounded part but had a light on the flat surface underneath. It was attached to the wall by crane like arms. They pulled it close to me. It was to my side, and as they raised it up above me the Grey who had spoken to me came up to me again. "Please, close your eyes", he insisted. I still did not obey his request. I wanted to see what they were doing. At that moment, the light on the device greatly intensified. I instantly closed my eyes in a natural reaction to the extreme white light emanating from it. I kept my eyes closed in fear that I would harm them should I open them. I lay still, not knowing what it was they were using this large machine for. Whatever they were doing with it did not cause me any discomfort. I felt nothing.

Since we were receiving so many answers from the Spirit Box that night that would lead one to believe that we had indeed achieved alien contact; I decided to really put it to the test and ask about my most recent abduction experience. I spoke as if I were speaking to the aliens, "you just took me and you used a device on me that I have never seen you use before." What was the device you used on me that you placed over my body?", I asked. A reply came back. "

Light tube", a voice said. I couldn't believe it! It made sense that they would call it a "light tube". That is exactly what it looked like. A tube of light cut in half. I assume that this large device with the bright light was possibly some kind of scanning instrument since it covered my entire body. All of us present for the Spirit Box session that night were shocked by the profound answers we heard. As has often been the case within the confines of the world of the paranormal and alien/UFO research, I was once again left with more questions than answers. Experiments like we conducted that night at Sandy Nichols' home with the Spirit Box opened up a myriad of possibilities along with a plethora of new questions.

Is it possible that because Sandy and I have implants placed in us by the Greys that they did know that we were going to attempt contact through the use of radio frequencies? Is it possible that the stoic computer sounding voices we heard replying to us were indeed just that? Aliens! Did the Greys use some kind of computer generated voice program to speak with us? I'm not in any way concluding that we were successful in our experiment. Nor am I emphatically stating that we were communicating with the Greys that night. I am, however, intrigued by the results of our experiment that night, to say the least, especially the information about the "light tube". If we weren't getting replies from the Greys, then how did the spirits know about the light tube? How did the spirits know how to correctly answer any of the questions we asked that night about Sandy and my abductions? To me, that is mind boggling within itself. Perhaps, if NASA or any other government organization around the world seeks to contact an alien civilization and/or species they should change their methodology. Maybe that realization reverts back to where it started when Nicola Tesla first proclaimed alien signals were coming through radio frequencies. One has to wonder if these random radio waves in combination with the implants in abductees are the key. There are many answers to pursue within the alien abduction phenomena, and I for one will keep seeking them and remain open to all possibilities.

I have often heard people say that they wish that aliens would abduct them. This disturbs me when I hear such talk. If only they truly understood what it is that they are wishing for, then I have no doubt that they would retract that wish. The trauma and psychological damage inflicted upon those of us unfortunate victims is undeniable. I wouldn't wish it on anyone. It is a painful and often lonely existence to live with. A secret hid from society only because of the fear of ridicule. I hope to help break the boundaries society has placed around this subject and in doing so help those who have also suffered at the hands of these visitors from another world. No one should have to suffer in silence as I did. I had always hoped that someday these strange creatures from another world would be done with me. I have given them much. When I got a vasectomy I thought that maybe that would end it; it didn't. I had hoped that I wouldn't be of any use to them as I reached middle age, but I have found out just how unrealistic these hopes of mine were. They keep coming for me no matter where I am, how old I am, or what I do to try to stop them. They just keep coming to take me. I have now succumbed to the fact that they will never stop taking me. I've come to accept it. I've learned to live with it; I have no choice. This is my life, my fate. It has been and will continue to be, never ending.

# Chapter 10

# The Agenda

It is my belief that, for many millenniums, aliens have been visiting earth. The evidence behind that statement is overwhelming. Many ancient texts, including the Bible, have reference after reference that would indicate that not only has our planet been visited by extraterrestrials but that they have had a direct influence on the progression of our species and some ancient texts (Sumerian for one) suggest that they even created homo-sapiens through DNA manipulation of pre-historic humans and their own which if true in essence makes us all alien hybrids. There are countless drawings, symbols, paintings and stone carvings left behind from many ancient cultures of what one could perceive as alien beings and alien spacecraft. There are stories passed down from generation to generation among many indigenous tribes through out the world of the ancestors who came from the stars. The evidence of human-alien interaction is very plausible and to me, undeniable. It has always been there, hidden in plain sight.

Given all this, the question of the alien agenda presents itself like the elephant in the room. So what is the real alien agenda? The answer to that age old question would depend on who you ask. Is there just one prime directive by all the alien visitors to this planet or are there many different agendas each pertaining to the individual alien species interacting or observing humans on earth? I've asked several of my friends who are all very well known and respected UFO researchers for their views on this complex subject which I am presenting here.

# The Alien Agenda

## By Kathleen Marden

*Kathleen Marden is a well-known UFO abduction researcher, author and lecturer with 23 years experience in the field. She is MUFON's Director of Abduction Research and FL MUFON's Director of Abduction Studies. For ten years Kathy volunteered as MUFON's Director of Field Investigator Training. In 2012, she was presented MUFON's "Ufologist of the Year" award.*

*She earned a B.A. degree in social work, with honors, from the University of New Hampshire in 1971, and participated in graduate studies in education while working as a teacher and education services coordinator. She is also a certified hypnotherapist.*

*Her interest in UFOs dates back to September 20, 1961, when her aunt, Betty Hill phoned her nearby home to report that she and Barney had encountered a flying saucer in New Hampshire's White*

*Mountains. A primary witness to the evidence of the UFO encounter and the aftermath, Kathleen has intimate knowledge of the Hill's biographical histories, personalities, and the previously unpublished historical files pertaining to their sensational story.*

*She is the author of three books, Captured! The Betty and Barney Hill UFO Experience, Science was Wrong, with nuclear physicist/scientific ufologist Stanton T. Friedman, and The Alien Abduction Files, with Denise Stoner (May 2013 release). Her chapter "UFO Abductions: Fact or Fiction" appears in UFOs and Aliens: Is There Anybody Out There?. Her articles have been published in the MUFON UFO Journal, Open Minds magazine and on several websites. Kathy has appeared in television and radio programs in the US, Canada and the UK, and has lectured throughout the United States.*

*Kathy resides with her family in Central Florida, and can be contacted at Kmarden@aol.com. Her mailing address is P.O. Box 120172, Clermont, FL 34712. You can purchase her books or read some of her articles at www.kathleen-marden.com .*

When Bret invited me to contribute a statement for his book regarding the perceived alien agenda, my first thought was that "experiencers" have described to me several agendas by a number of prominent ET groups. I had recently completed a yearlong research project designed to identify commonalities among abduction experiencers which gave me additional insight into the perceived alien agenda. (See "Commonalities Study Final Report" at www.kathleen-marden.com)

Participants in the study mentioned contact with several ET types, including 3 ½ to 4 foot tall Greys, 4 ½ to 5 foot taller Greys, Insectoid praying mantis types, Reptilians, and human types (such as Nordics, Annunaki, and late stage hybrids). A tiny percentage of the respondents mentioned less prevalent groups, such as tall whites, goldens, and browns, short, pudgy blues, and Yeti types. The most prevalent group in this study is Grey non-human entities. Anecdotal reports suggest that the Grey and Insectoid groups are working cooperatively with one another on medical experiments and education involving humans. Space limitations make it impossible for me to discuss all of the different perceived agendas, so I will state simply that the most positive experience reports were with Nordic types (highly spiritual, benevolent, compassionate), and the most negative accounts came from individuals that claimed abductions by Reptilians (cruel, insensitive).

For the purpose of this paper, I will focus primarily upon what I have learned from abduction experiencers about the Grey's perceived agenda. Certainly it is impossible to voice an unequivocal opinion pertaining to this subject matter, as it comes primarily from the subjective experiences of individuals, but a quantitative analysis of experiencers' responses increases one's chance of finding valid information. It is fortuitous, in my opinion, that some experiencers retain conscious, continuous recall of at least part of their abduction experience and have eye witnesses, plus circumstantial evidence. Eighty-eight percent of the respondents in "The Marden-Stoner Study on Commonalities among Abduction Experiencers" had conscious recall of at least one abduction experience and were not alone when it occurred. More than two thirds observed a craft at less than a thousand feet, and fifty-six percent saw non-human entities prior to at least one abduction experience. In addition to this, more than sixty percent had witnesses with conscious recall for at least part of the experience.

It becomes increasingly difficult when information is retrieved exclusively through hypnosis, unless there are additional witnesses whose independent testimony, under hypnosis, confirms the detailed memories of the first witness. This is because hypnotic subjects have a propensity to confabulate fantasy material when no real memories exist, especially when they are asked to recall details. Only thirty-eight percent of the study's participants had undergone hypnosis to facilitate recall. The fact that the vast majority of participants had conscious recall of some of their experiences strengthens the validity of their testimony about the alien agenda.

Taken together with a March 2012 article that appeared in Life Science magazine, I have gained additional insight into what I and others perceive to be the Grey's agenda. The article spoke of a U.S. military plan developed during the 1950's that outlined the seven steps to contact we would take if we discovered intelligent life elsewhere. (1) By all accounts, it appears that our alien visitors are following similar protocols. Step one would begin with remote surveillance and data gathering and eventually move toward close approaches, to determine whether or not the planet's inhabitants are hostile. Frank C. Feschino, Jr.'s book Shoot The Down: The Flying Saucer Air Wars of 1952 lists case after case of aerial encounters during the summer of 1952 where U.S. fighter planes were on 24 hour nationwide alert to "shoot them down" if they refused to land. This documented evidence indicates that our alien visitors have every reason to perceive us as hostile.

Steps four and five include securing plant and animal specimens and the abduction of intelligent beings. It brings to mind the many historical reports of landed UFOs with their occupants collecting "soil samples". The abduction of intelligent beings by non-humans is well documented in several compelling evidence reports dating back to 1957. (Villa Boas, Betty and Barney Hill, Buff Ledge, Hickson/Parker, Travis Walton, Smith/Stafford/Thomas, Allagash, Romanek, etc.) Thousands of humans have reported being taken into an alien environment where they were subjected to intrusive physical examinations, mind scans, images of cataclysmic events, the acquisition of advanced knowledge, and sometimes healings. It occurs around the world across racial, cultural, religious, educational, and economic lines.

Unexplained marks, such as patterned bruises, scoop marks, puncture wounds, sunburn-like redness, and rashes are commonly reported by abduction experiencers. A highly significant eighty-three percent of the abduction experiencer participants in the commonalities study stated that they had awoken with unexplained marks on their bodies, whereas only twenty percent of the control group replied in the affirmative. Long, thin bruises (like finger marks), were most often found on women's calves or thighs, suggesting that a reproductive procedure had transpired. Often the women remembered at least part of the procedure. Scoop marks (tissue samples), were most commonly reported near elbows, ankles, and behind knees. Puncture wounds were often found on hands and rib cages. Several men believed that tissue had been extracted from their thymus gland (a specialized organ of the immune system). A few experiencers were released with patterned burn marks on their shoulders or necks and sunburn like rashes. Over fifty percent of the experiencer group stated that they experienced nosebleeds immediately after an abduction experience. Several stated that their physicians had been concerned about significant scarring in their nasal cavities. One mentioned that his physician found a strange metal object (presumably a tracking device), high in his nasal passage and another told of expelling a suspected implant from her nose the day after an abduction experience.

A significant sixty-nine percent of the female experiencers reported gynecological abnormalities, whereas only a third of the control group made the same report. This statistic offers compelling evidence of an increased percentage of gynecological problems among abduction experiencers purportedly as the direct result of reproductive procedures performed on them by non-humans. Two respondents from the experiencer group mentioned that they had tested positive for pregnancy, but following an abduction found that they were no longer pregnant, and there had been no cramping or bleeding. Both recalled observing fetuses purportedly being gestated in tubes on craft and hybrid baby presentations. Some believe that they have carried genetically altered fetuses to full term.

Illnesses that might be generated by the stress, related to alien abduction, were reported by a significant percentage of the experiencers. Forty percent stated that they suffer from migraine headaches, although only eight percent of the control group does. Thirty-eight percent reported Chronic Fatigue and Immune Dysfunction Syndrome or reactivating mononucleosis diagnosis, whereas less than one percent of the general population has CFIDS. This is a highly significant finding.

When we combine this with our discovery that nearly three quarters of the experiencer group had difficulty falling asleep and staying asleep, we have to question whether or not this is the result of post traumatic stress disorder stemming from the abduction experience. It is interesting to note that sleep quality improved when experiencers overcame their fear of alien abduction.

One can raise a speculative argument that illnesses among experiencers are caused by the procurement process, when abductees are moved through solid surfaces, by the alien environment, or by the Grey's experiments. It has been reported by some experiencers that the Greys have attempted to raise their vibrational frequencies either as a healing process or for transport.

Despite the constellation of medical symptoms common among abduction experiencers, there have been some positive outcomes reported. Half of the participants in the Marden-Stoner Commonalities Study stated that they were able to heal others for at least a short period following an abduction experience. This gift persisted for an extended period of time for some of the participants, but not for others. I have received numerous anecdotal reports from individuals that claim to have been healed during an abduction experience.

It is interesting that nearly three quarters stated that they are more sensitive or intuitive than they were prior to contact and nearly eight percent stated that they had developed new psychic abilities after a contact experience. Additionally, eighty-eight percent reported that they had witnessed paranormal activity in their homes, such as light orbs that dart or float through the air and poltergeist activity.

Sixth in our military's seven steps to contact are low level approaches to make our presence known. This brings to mind the gigantic carpenter's square shaped craft sited over Arizona, Nevada and Senora, Mexico, that was observed by thousands of witnesses on March 13, 1997. Its "otherworldly" appearance and flight pattern was initially covered up by Arizona's governor, Fyfe Symington, but later revealed by him. On November 7, 2006, a dozen employees, including pilots and supervisors at Chicago's O'Hare Airport and several witnesses outside the airport, observed a low level approach by a disk-shaped object that hovered over gate C-17. Close approaches by unconventional aerial craft are being reported to the Mutual UFO network on a fairly consistent basis. One has to pause and consider the possibility that our ET visitors are weighing the pros and cons of implementing the eighth step: Overt Contact.

One must ask, "Are we a species that can accept overt contact without suffering too many negative consequences?" Or would people from around the world experience fear and a sense of complete powerlessness? Would the world experience ontological shock so great that governments, public institutions, and economic endeavors would collapse, at least temporarily? Would media outlets engage in fear mongering to increase their ratings without easing the public's fears? Given the many human concerns that arise when we consider the consequences of overt contact one has to hope that our Grey visitors (and others), are sensitive enough to protect our primitive, warlike species until we move ahead on an evolutionary scale.

Consider the idea that the Greys are significantly different than humans. Their communication style is telepathic. Their physical structure is reportedly different than ours, suggesting that they are a non-mammalian species. We are told that they have the ability to pass through solid surfaces and can enter locked buildings at will. By all appearances they are an ancient, highly developed species. Perhaps they are so different than humans that overt interaction would be impossible. Or perhaps they don't want to be held accountable for their behavior toward us. They know that we might possibly attempt to defend our planet from a perceived invasion by them. It follows that their only options would be to engage in warfare against us, possibly resulting in our destruction, or leave our planet and the human experimental subjects that have been a part of their grand longitudinal study. Given the possible negative consequences of overt contact, it seems that their current policy of covert interaction has served them well.

Notes:

(1) Natalie Wolchover, "If We Discover Aliens, What's Our Protocol for Making Contact?" March 29, 2012. LifeScience.com

# The Alien Agenda

# By Brad Steiger

*The author/co-author of 170 books, Brad Steiger wrote the paper-back bestseller Strangers from the Skies about UFOs. His edited work Project Bluebook was hailed by Omni magazine as one of the best UFO books of the century. Steiger was inducted into the Hypnosis Hall of Fame for his work with UFO contactees, abduct-ees, and past life regression. In Minneapolis, he received the Lifetime Achievement Award at the National UFO and Unexplained Phenomena Conference.*

*The author/co-author of 43 books, Brad's wife, Sherry Steiger, an ordained minister with a special interest in UFOs in the Bible and world religions, began working closely in 1985 with Dr. J. Allen Hynek, official scientific advisor for the U.S. Air Force's twenty-year study of UFOs. Sherry served as his publicist, and confidante at his nonprofit UFO research organization in Phoenix until his death in 1986. This position made her privy to unpub-lished research and more than 80,000 documented cases from 161 countries.*

*For many decades, the Steigers have researched and investi-gated UFOs and their cultural impact throughout world history, and they have lectured and conducted seminars on the phenomenon throughout the United States and overseas. Sherry and Brad were featured in twenty-two episodes of the television series Could It Be a Miracle? Together, their television appearances and specials include: The Joan Rivers Show, Entertainment Tonight, Inside Edition, Hard Copy, Hollywood Insider, and specials on HBO, USA Network, The Learning Channel, The History Channel, and Arts and Entertainment (A&E), among others. They appear frequently as guests on numerous domestic and international radio talk shows.*

I have been engaged in UFO research since the early 1950's, and I have come to the conclusion that, throughout history, some external intelligence has interacted with Homo sapiens in an effort to learn more about us--or in an effort to communicate to our spe-cies certain basic truths. I am also convinced that a subtle kind of symbiotic relationship exists between humankind and the UFO intelligences. I believe that, in a way which we have yet to deter-mine, they need us as much as we need them. It is quite possible that either or both species might once have had a common extrater-restrial origin; but most important, it may be that the very biologi-cal and spiritual evolution of Earth depends upon the establishment of equilibrium between us and our cosmic cousins.

I do not dogmatically exclude the extraterrestrial hypothesis, but I prefer the theory that UFOs may be our neighbors, right around the corner in another Space-Time continuum.

One day an alien astronaut from an extraterrestrial world may indeed request a startled Earthling to take him to his leader. However, what we have thus far been labeling "spaceships," I believe to be multidimensional mechanisms or psychic constructs of our paraphysical companions. I have even come to suspect that, in some instances, what we have been calling "spaceships" may actually be a form of higher intelligences rather than vehicles trans-porting occupants.

I feel, too, that these paraphysical beings have the ability to influence the human mind telepathically in order to project what may appear to be three-dimensional images. The image seen may depend in large part upon the preconceptions the human observer has about alien life forms. Thus reported accounts of spaceship occupants run the gamut from Bug-Eyed Monsters, to little Green Men, to Metaphysical Space Brothers.

Although we may not perceive these intelligences in their true form--if, indeed, they even possess physical forms--it seems clear that most people would be readier to communicate with a "Visitor" that is fairly conventional in appearance, and that once human attention has been attracted, the UFO intelligence-mechanism could quite easily alter human consciousness. I believe that many of the "chance" encounters that occur between human witnesses and the Other are in reality learning experiences for the human percipients; that is, they were designed to assist the percipients to become aware that humankind is not alone in the universe or on this planet.

Although the messages relayed by UFO entities are always relevant to the time context of human observers, the form in which the UFO construct appears, and the symbology it employs, is always timeless, archetypal, and instantly recognizable at one level of the percipient's consciousness. Elves, fairies, genies, and wee people, it would seem, have been popular in all cultures throughout history.

Skeptics always question why schoolboys, nurses, electrical engineers, and salesmen should serve as witnesses of interactions with UFO intelligences. Why, the cynic asks, should the UFO entities not manifest themselves to scientists, government officials, politicians, or military men. The answer is that the UFO intelligences have appeared to every category of human kind. After extensive research, I have come to the conclusion that it may not really matter who perceives the UFO intelligences, the important thing is that someone sees and interacts with them on either a conscious or an unconscious level.

If there is but one Life Force and a common, collective unconscious for Homo sapiens, then, in the larger sense, any contact with UFO intelligences becomes part of the common experience of all mankind, whether the incident is reported in the popular press or pondered quietly in the mind of the individual observer.

To me, the UFO, the appearance of elves and wee people, and the manifestation of archetypal images throughout the world signify that we are part of a larger community of intelligences, a far more complex hierarchy of powers and principalities, a potentially richer kingdom of interrelated species-both physical and nonphysical-than we have been bold enough to believe.

In my book Mysteries of Time and Space, I suggested that some undeclared paraphysical opponents have engaged our species in what I call the Reality Game. When we have apprehended the true significance of this contest, we will attain such control of our life and our abilities that we will confront all aspects of existence with the same ease and freedom with which we would enter a game. I believe that this is a glorious way to approach life, truly reflective of humankind's noble, star-seeded heritage. And the rewards of truly understanding what I have come to call the Reality Game are greater than we have dared to envision.

Once we have correctly fathomed the meaning of The Other and its total relevance to our lives, we will perceive how an evolved Intelligence, whose manifestations we have been mistakenly labeling our "gods," has been challenging us, teaching us, and preparing us to recognize fully the "god-self" within each one of us. Throughout the centuries of humankind's spiritual and intellectual evolution the UFO has become a living mythological symbol designed to waken and to give guidance to the energies of life

The distinguished scholar Joseph Campbell has observed that the most important function of such a mythological symbol not only "turns a person on," but it turns him in a specific direction which enables him to participate effectively in a functioning social group.

Dr. John W. Perry has identified the living mythological symbol as an "affect image"--an image which speaks directly to the feeling system and instantly elicits a response. Only after the image has affected the percipient where it really counts does the brain provide interpretive and appreciative comments. If a symbol must first be "read" by the brain, it is already a dead symbol and will not produce a responding resonance within the percipient, ... like the answer of a musical string to another equally tuned." When the vital symbols of any given social group are able to evoke such resonances within all its members, ". . . a sort of magical accord unites them as one spiritual organism, functioning through members, who, though separate in space, are yet one in being and belief."

It is my contention that the UFO continues to provide contemporary humans with a vital, living mythological symbol, an "affect image," which communicates directly to our essential selves, bypassing our brains, evading acculturation, manipulating historical conditioning. I believe that the UFO will somehow serves humankind as a transformative symbol that will unite our entire species as one spiritual organism, functioning through members, who, though separate in space, are yet one in being and belief."

To suggest that the UFO is a living mythological symbol does not diminish its reality in an objective, physical sense. Indeed, the UFO may ultimately be more real than the transitory realities of computers, machines, associations, political parties, or détentes. Through the cosmic catharsis of dreams, visions, and inspirations, the UFO will serve as the spiritual midwife that will bring about humankind's starbirth into the universe.

# My Personal Reflections on the Alien Agenda

## By Brent Raynes

*Brent Raynes, the author of Visitors from Hidden Realms (2004) and On The Edge of Reality (2009), is the editor of Alternate Perceptions magazine (http://apmagazine.info/) and the host of Alternate Perceptions blogtalk radio (http://www.liveparanormal.com/). Brent has been studying UFOs and other forms of high-strangeness (essentially anything paranormal) since he was 14, going back to early 1967. Since 1985, Brent has worked for the Tennessee Department of Correction, is married, has a daughter, and four grandkids. He can be reached at: BrentRaynes@yahoo.com.*

Undoubtedly, attempting to discern the proverbial truth behind the presumed alien agenda is certainly at the very heart of the complex and controversial alien abduction/contactee syndrome. No doubt this represents ufology's greatest challenge. Logic alone would indeed seem to dictate that investigators should diligently pursue the close encounter cases because one could infer from such evidence that increased opportunities to acquire more detailed and meaningful data existed. Distant and odd behaving lights and shapes in the sky make for interesting reports, but they offer very limited insight, understanding and interpretation into the nature of what is being observed. However, with close encounters and contact case histories we have much more information to work with. In some cases, we even have reported physical trace effects (i.e., unexplained body marks on witnesses, circular patterns on the ground where a UFO reportedly landed, etc.).

The body of evidence is quite impressive. Thousands of sane and sober appearing men and women, from all walks of life, and from all over the world, have now shared their personal accounts of these close UFO/alien encounters. There are many consistent similarities to be found again and again in these strange incidents.

However, surface appearances can be misleading and may largely reflect ones belief systems based upon whatever level of social, cultural, and religious perspectives that may exist at whatever time period we may be talking about. In reality, remarkably similar reports can be found going back many centuries, well before our modern "flying saucer" era which began in 1947. For example, a number of ufologists have concluded that many alien encounters are actually intelligent beings known to the Muslim world as the Jinn (also spelled Djinn by some, and best known to us from Muslim folklore as a jinni called up from rubbing a magic lamp). "These creatures, the Jinns of the Muslim religion and the elementals in the Buddhist religion, reportedly can materialize and dematerialize, and so can our Western culture's abducting creatures," long-time California author and UFO investigator Ann Druffel told me. "They shape-shift in various forms, they delight in harassing and traumatizing human beings. They reportedly abduct human beings and transport them long distances in a matter of seconds. And the Jinns, the elementals, and our own abducting Greys [have taken] a sexual interest in human beings down through the millennia. In every major culture of the world, and in many minor cultures, they all have those same folkloric stories, and even religious and philosophical texts in some of the countries talk about this 'third order of creation,' as the Muslims call it. They aren't angels, they aren't devils, they aren't human beings. They're something in between that share our world with us in a hidden state."

An admitted religious agnostic turned historical religious scholar of sorts, noted UFO author/investigator John Keel concluded years ago that ufologists studying the contactee syndrome were pursuing "a hallucinatory world of 'devil's marks' and classic demonological manifestations."

"The landings, abductions and contacts and general tomfoolery are primarily part of a very ancient, very well observed phenomenon that has spawned all of man's belief systems," Keel wrote. "It has no more basis in reality than the popular Arab belief in Djinns. The manifestations behind these systems have a purpose that has been deliberately hidden from the human race for thousands of years."

Thomas E. Bullard, Ph.D., a noted American folklorist, reported specific similarities between modern UFO "abduction" cases and the earlier accounts of so-called fairy kidnappings, initiation ordeals, and shamanic spirit journeys to the land of the dead. Bullard wrote: "The initiation vision of a Siberian shaman presents an especially vivid example: While lying in a comatose state for hours or days the candidate meets two friendly spirits who escort him into the underworld. Unfriendly spirits then dismember the candidate and reconstruct his body with new powers added, including rock crystals, all with magical powers inserted into the head. The candidate spends part of his stay inside a domed cave with uniform but source less lighting, and returns to his home a changed man, with new abilities and a new vocation. How closely these incidents resemble the abduction time lapse, escort, examination, inserts, examination room, and life changes needs no further comment. ... The abduction story is not so unique after all."

It does seem that when we take a comprehensive global and historical appraisal of the UFO abduction/contactee syndrome that striking parallels and remarkable similarities do indeed emerge from many widely diverse and seemingly unrelated sources.

In the early part of our modern UFO era sceptics easily dismissed the extraterrestrial visitation theory by knowingly pointing out the obvious fact that stars with habitable planets had to be many light years away and even if they could travel at the speed of light, it would still be too great a distance for such visitors to be cavorting through our skies as easily and frequently as gets reported by UFO witnesses, and besides, where's all those crashed saucers (besides in some super-secret storage facility at Wright Patterson Air Force Base)?

However, a glimmer of progress can be acknowledged as many scientists today talking about quantum physics, of worm holes and other dimensions of existence, have opened up a renewed and serious theoretical discussion on all of this that goes along fairly well with current scientific thinking, as well as the concept some creative ufologists have advanced over the years to explain why UFOs come and go as frequently as they do and never seem to get caught up with and leave behind anything truly substantial evidence-wise. The scientist's string theories, worm hole theories and all such exotic and esoteric sounding theories of quantum science are appearing just as far out as anything any imaginative ufologist could ever hope to express. Nonetheless, most scientists still prefer to steer well clear of being involved in the UFO controversy for the same old reason that they've always avoided this subject. Simply put, it's a career buster being affiliated with members of what is still largely dismissed as the "lunatic fringe" by the majority of mainstream scientists, even if, as one physicist who has studied paranormal phenomena in the laboratory setting put it recently (I'm going to paraphrase here): there's more proof for psychic phenomena than string theory!

Whatever we're dealing with in regard to this so-called "alien agenda," a very important point in dealing effectively with the challenges and complexity of all of this high-strangeness is to try and maintain a personal clarity of mind and focus ourselves (Bret recommends meditation), which can prove especially challenging in light of the apparent "mixed bag" of alien types and motives that seem to exist. Nonetheless, we certainly do need to make certain that our own focus and intent is what it should be.

Over the past three years of having the distinct pleasure and honour of personally knowing Bret and his wife Gina, and participating in dozens of paranormal/UFO field investigations with them, I have come to better understand and more fully appreciate the positive dynamics of the power of good intention and focus.

# The Alien Agenda: My Personal Beliefs

## By Sandy Nichols

*Sandy's involvement in the paranormal stems from his own personal experiences that began when he was just a young child of five. In 1996 he formed the "Alien Research Group" (www.alienresearchgroup.com) not just to uncover the truth behind his involvement, but to help others as well. In the ensuing years, he has garnered a high degree of respect among his peers for his honesty and credibility through his writings, research and investigations. Throughout the years, Sandy has worked closely with others in the field, most notably Bret and Gina Oldham, Brent and Joan Raynes, Chandra Harrison, and Janice Edwards. Sandy considers it a great honor and privilege when asked to contribute to other researchers and investigator's works.*

When I was first asked by Bret if I would like to contribute something for his new book expressing my beliefs as to the agenda behind "Alien Abductions," I immediately replied "Yes!" And felt honored for this privilege. Writing something about this type of agenda can be a bit tricky though. For an agenda to be formulated, there must be an ideology behind it, usually conceived by one person and then eventually accepted by others. Sometimes when sharing ones beliefs on the alien agenda, it is not unheard of to encounter someone who is intolerant of your beliefs. They have gotten to the point where, to them, your beliefs are foolish and stupid, and their beliefs are right. For me, it is not much different than hearing one person slam another person for differing religious beliefs. I would imagine that most of us have all heard or personally experienced something similar in our own lives at some time.

But what happens if intolerance for differing beliefs is interwoven into a national agenda? A nation's political agenda is based upon the political party that runs that nation, and that political party will establish agendas based on specific ideologies. These agendas are touted as being for the good of the nation and/or the world, but oftentimes can actually do more harm than good. And what if a nation's political agenda is also based upon a religious ideology as well?

Back in the 16th Century, Spain was a powerful nation that sent its fleet far and wide to expand their empire and exert its dominance. By doing so, they also hoped to find gold, silver and other riches in newly discovered lands to be sent back to fill their coffers at home. But Spain was also a very religious nation and influenced greatly by the Roman Catholic Church. There was never a ship that left Spain on a voyage without at least one Catholic priest onboard. The purpose of the priest was three-fold: to establish a foothold by building missions and churches, conversion of the indigenous population to the Catholic faith and also to bring back riches to fill the church coffers. If there were any type of resistance to this agenda, then it was legal by Spanish and church law to exterminate the resistors and destroy anything deemed heathen or pagan. This was never more so than the Spanish Conquest of Central and South America. Thousands of years of Mayan, Aztec, Toltec and Olmec history were destroyed in less than a century. Not any one of the early Spanish explorers such as Columbus, Cortez, Ponce de Leon, or de Soto can be singled out alone for this travesty. By all accounts, they were very devoted and deeply religious men abiding by the dictates of the Spanish Crown and the Catholic Church. In ignorance, they were simply following an agenda that was established and believed to be for the good.

For myself personally, I feel that the greatest loss as a result of the Spanish Conquest came from the destruction and suppression of these ancient nation's religious beliefs. Anything the Spanish believed to be evil was destroyed. Priest and shamans were killed along with the knowledge they possessed. Any and all written records were destroyed except a few documents that were quickly spirited and hidden away when the destruction and extermination began. Great religious temples and pyramids were torn down, and Catholic Churches or towns were built on top of the ruins. A good example of this is modern day Mexico City, which was built on the ruins of the Aztec capital.

One of the main religious beliefs was the worship of the same god or deity that was similarly described back to the first century BC, although there is Stella 19 of the Olmec culture showing a similar god or deity rising up behind a shaman dating to 900 BC. The name of this god most known by us today is Aztec "Quetzalcoatl," or the Mayan name "Kukulcan." Though the name itself might be different for each successive culture, the physical description of this god is basically the same as well as what this god looked like and is known for. He is described as being a winged, feathered serpent or snake who descended from the sky. He is sometimes depicted as being somewhat humanoid looking as well. I find this very interesting in that today many abductees, including myself, have stated that one of the species of aliens that abducts us are "The Reptilians." I find it very interesting as well that Quetzalcoatl along with his twin, Tezcatlipoca, were supposed to be the gods of creation and givers of life. This duality of a male/female creator god is contradictory to the Judeo-Christian faith, but the creation part follows along a similar belief. It is easy to understand why these ancient cultures worshiped Quetzalcoatl as a god. His powers would have seemed to have been magical or god like. The Aztec and other cultures aligned him with the wind and the planet Venus. Would it be a stretch to imagine that if he were an ET, that the engines from his space craft created strong currents of air when in use, and that maybe he landed in the early morning hours when Venus was high and bright in the early morning sky? If this were the case, then it might not be too hard to imagine that his twin could have been another ET. Once out of their craft, the ETs with their advance knowledge and technology could have easily been mistaken for gods. At the same time if one ET was a lower rank than the other ET and taking orders, then this might explain why Quetzalcoatl is the more prominent of the two gods. It is also said that Quetzalcoatl physically ruled over selected city states which would have been a logical place for ETs to live during their time on earth instead of being cooped up in a space craft.

Being such a powerful god, Quetzalcoatl was revered as the patron god of the Aztec priestly caste whose knowledge of construction, planting, astronomy, math, music and language he bestowed upon the priests. The worship of Quetzalcoatl was such that, throughout the centuries his image as a feathered serpent, snake or human was carved in the stones of many structures, especially religious and astronomical temples. Quetzalcoatl was also linked to the "Underworld," or "The Land of the Dead" which we will see later was also very important in other, far distant lands and cultures, most notably, Egypt.

Over time, a dark side also emerged in the worship of Quetzalcoatl that to the invading Spaniards seemed barbaric and evil and surely of the devil that must be destroyed...human sacrifice. Many of these sacrifices were of defeated and captured enemies, but during other ceremonies a sacrificial virgin would be offered up, which, to the virgin, would be an honor to die for the gods. I find this sense of barbarism and evil rather ironic considering how many people have been murdered and tortured in the name of the biblical God.

Before moving on there is one more interesting aspect of the worship of Quetzalcoatl that I must mention here that takes on a more modern tone. In the Book of Mormon it is believed that after Jesus' resurrection he visited the Americas. Some Mormons believe that Quetzalcoatl was, in fact, Jesus, a white, bearded man who came from the sky and promised to return. Mormons are not alone in this belief. There are legends from other cultures that humanoid like beings descended from the sky and imparted wisdom and guidance among the inhabitants and departed with a promise to return one day.

As I stated earlier the worship of a winged, feathered, serpent being was not confined to just Mesoamerica. Other cultures, most notably Egypt, also had their own version and variation of a winged, serpent type god. Thoth was one of the most important Egyptians gods in the multitude of Egyptian gods. He is depicted in two ways: either with the head of a bird or the head of a baboon. Thoth was always depicted as holding a "Was (rod or wand)" in one hand symbolizing "Power," and an "Ankh" in the other hand symbolizing "Life." Like Quetzalcoatl, Thoth had a twin named Seshat. Seshat was the goddess of wisdom, knowledge and writing. Later in history she was identified as the goddess of building, astronomy, astrology, and math. Another name for Seshat was "Mistress of the House of Books." In this capacity she was the deity that guided the priest who oversaw the library where the most important knowledge was stored as well as magical secrets. Thoth was a very powerful god whose purpose in life was to maintain the universe in a balance between opposing forces. He was also one half of a whole with his wife Ma'at being the other half who was also very powerful. One of their duties was to stand on either side of Ra's Boat which represents the sun (solar) deity or sky deity in male/female form. While Thoth maintained the universe, Ma'at was the goddess who regulated the stars and the seasons, and she was the mediator between the people and the gods while Thoth was the mediator between the gods themselves. Both Thoth and Ma'at played integral parts in the "Judgment of the Dead." As with Thoth, Ma'at was depicted with a Was in one hand and an Ankh in the other denoting not just a duality but also an equality between the two. Ma'at also wore a feather in a headband which was supposed to weigh the souls of the dead. I also wonder if the feather was in some way a symbolic connection to Quetzalcoatl the feathered serpent god.

As one can see there are many similarities between Quetzalcoatl and Thoth, but there are two main differences as well. Where Thoth and Ma'at as twins worked together in balance, Quetzalcoatl and his twin Tezcatlipoca were rivals, with Tezcatlipoca being considered a male deity. Scientists and archeologists tell us that this rivalry/duality is only symbolic and represents a primitive culture trying to understand the difference between night and day... Symbolic in the sense of a war being fought between the sun and the moon and stars...in other words, a continuous cycle of life that never ends. The temples and pyramids built to the gods were simply burial chambers for the kings, sacrificial altars to the gods, or astronomical platforms to determine the different planting seasons. Scientists and archeologists refuse to even consider that these gods could have been real, other world beings trying to help humans along their evolutionary journey.

As one delves further into human history, one can see that Mesoamerica and Egypt were not the only cultures that had gods, legends and myths about sky gods descending to earth. The Greek historian Herodotus discusses Greek gods and compares them in similarity to Egyptian gods. Zeus' counterpart was the Egyptian god Amun. The Egyptian god, Thoth, was the counterpart to the Greek god, Hermes. The male Egyptian god, Osiris, was the counterpart to the Greek god, Dionysus. Io, the Greek Priestess god was the counterpart to the Egyptian god, Isis. Isis was the goddess of nature and magic, and like Ma'at, carried in her hands the Was and Ankh. It is also interesting that Isis was the "Protector of the Dead," which should make one wonder about her relationship with Thoth and Ma'at and their control of the Underworld or Afterlife.

Now what is not clear and debated is why Herodotus identified Egyptian gods with Greek gods. Some scholars argue that Herodotus did this so the Greek people could claim these powerful gods as their own. Others contend that Herodotus was attempting to show that although both cultures had similar gods that each god from both cultures had evolved separately from each other. In other words, the Greeks did not claim the Egyptian gods as their own. This makes one wonder if these gods did, in fact, evolve separately from each other. Then what unknown or hidden factor link the two cultures together to have such similar gods? This same unknown or hidden factor could also link Quetzalcoatl and the Egyptian and Greek gods together all in one bundle as well. If an assumption could be made for an ET interaction in Mesoamerica, could this same assumption be made that contends that the same ET's or other ET's of the same species could have spread out around the earth and interacted with other humans at the same time? If so, then this interaction with humans would have surely have been a grand agenda formulated and put into action by an advanced ET species. At the time this agenda was undertaken, one would assume that such an agenda was a good thing to help humans evolve, but listening to many abductees share today, there seems to be the distinct possibility that somewhere down the road the agenda changed from its original good intent.

In order to better understand how wide spread around the world these particular gods were I think it is wise if we take a quick look at some of these other cultures and their gods.

There are several Roman gods that have very similar traits and attributes of the gods I have discussed already. At the top of the Roman god list was Jupiter who was looked upon as the "King of the gods." The Greek equivalent was Zeus. Jupiter's main defense was lightning and thunder, which interestingly enough is what greeted Moses on top of Mt. Sinai where he received the Ten Commandments from the biblical God. Next in line was Juno, "Queen of the gods." She was the wife of Jupiter, and even though all gods feared Jupiter, Jupiter at times feared of Juno. Next up was Neptune, whose is associated with the Greek god, Poseidon. Neptune was the brother of Jupiter, and the "God of the Sea." It is interesting to note here that several ancient texts talk of a group of people simply called "The Sea People and or the Sea gods." Even though, very little is known about the Sea People, many scholars agree that they must have existed as real people. Going on the down the line is the Roman God, Pluto. Pluto was the god of the "Underworld/Hades/Hell." It is very interesting to note here that once someone died they first journeyed to the Underworld. The coins placed on their eyes were to pay the boatman, Charon, to carry them across the River of the Dead; or another name, Styx. Once across the river they were confronted by a multi-headed dog with snake like features, that was created out of an union between a mortal and a serpent, called Ceberus, that guarded the gates of Hell and only let the dead pass. Once past Ceberus, the dead faced the Judges of the

Dead who were the three mortal sons of Zeus who became demigods, and who judged the sins of the dead.

The last Roman god I want to mention is Mercury, whose Greek equivalent was, Hermes. Mercury was used as a "Messenger of the gods," as well as a god of science and business. He was cunning and fleet of foot, and sometimes a bit mischievous. One of his godly gifts was his ability to fly which is represented by wings either on his shoes or hat. In his hand he carries a staff or "Caduceus" which also has wings and two intertwining snakes wrapped around it. This caduceus was adopted as a symbol of medicine by the U. S. Army Medical Corp in 1902, and variations of the caduceus has been adopted as the main symbol for anything associated with medical/ healthcare. The caduceus is also used at times as a symbol for business and or commerce.

Various oral traditions have the Dogon people of West Africa migrating from different regions to eventually settling in the country of Mali around the 15th Century. The Dogon people today embrace the Muslim religion, but hold steadfastly to other non-traditional religious beliefs firmly established and believed for a couple of thousand years. And very much like the other cultures where their gods descended from the sky, so too did the main Dogon god in a craft accompanied by lightning and thunder. But there is a major physical difference between the Dogon gods and the winged, feathered serpent gods. The Dogon sky gods were amphibious in nature being described as half man from the waist up, and half fish from the waist down but also with a pair of legs. The Dogon called these amphibious, sky gods, "The Nommo," and later they were also referred to as "The Sea People and The Sea Gods." These gods mingled with the population during the day and imparted wisdom and knowledge, but at night they descended to the watery depths of the sea. One of the most controversial aspects of the Dogon culture is their knowledge of astronomy. Somehow the Dogon's knowledge was such that they knew about the rings of Saturn and the moons of Jupiter. Long before the advent of telescopes and satellites, the Dogon spoke of a triple star system known as Sirius A and B. Skeptics claimed that the Dogon just made up the fact that Sirius was a triple star system because science knew that it was only a Binary star system. Then in 1995 with the aid of modern scientific equipment, astronomers conducting gravity wave experiments announced the very real possibility that Sirius could very well indeed be a triple star system. This did not dissuade the skeptics contention that there was no possible way the Dogon could have known this. Their answer to this perplexing dilemma was that the Dogon acquired this information from outside, human sources and then integrated it into their own Nommo religious beliefs. These same skeptics also stated that the Nommo god was nothing more than allegoric tales to explain away mysteries that they could not explain. This sounds very much like what the skeptics say about the winged, feathered serpent gods of other cultures.

Now for those with limited knowledge about ancient cultures, and believing that human history is exactly the way it was taught to us in school, one might side with the skeptics that there was never an amphibious, ET species that interacted with the Dogons, unless one studies the history of ancient Babylon.

The Babylonians were an exceptional culture that lived in modern day, Iraq. A great deal of what we consider intellectual and scientific knowledge originated from this great culture. Babylon was in its hey-day, the biggest and baddest boy on the block. Their armies conquered much of the then known world, and they brought back ancient knowledge from conquered territories and housed it in the magnificent Babylon library. This library of knowledge was so extensive that it rivaled the great library at Alexandria, Egypt. Like other cultures, Babylon had its share of gods, and one Babylonian god was called "EA," or in the Greek, "Oannes," but with some debate about the origin of the names.

Like the Dogon god, Nommo, Oannes was an amphibious god as well with a similarly described appearance, the only difference being that he emerged from the sea instead of descending from the sky. He still possessed god like powers, lived among the people and imparted wisdom to the population and at night returned to the sea.

The Babylonian writer, Berossus, wrote the following about Oannes:

"At first they led a somewhat wretched existence and lived without rule after the manner of beasts. But, in the first year appeared an animal endowed with human reason, named Oannes, who rose from out of the Erythian Sea, at the point where it borders Babylonia. He had the whole body of a fish, but above his fish's head he had another head which was that of a man, and human feet emerged from beneath his fish's tail. He had a human voice, and an image of him is preserved unto this day. He passed the day in the midst of men without taking food; he taught them the use of letters, sciences and arts of all kinds. He taught them to construct cities, to found temples, to compile laws, and explained to them the principles of geometrical knowledge. He made them distinguish the seeds of the earth, and showed them how to collect the fruits; in short he instructed them in everything which could tend to soften human manners and humanize their laws. From that time, nothing material has been added by way of improvement to his instructions. And when the sun set, this being Oannes, retired again into the sea, for he was amphibious. After this, there appeared other animals like Oannes."

The Discovery Channel recently aired a very intriguing documentary about Mermaids that told of myths, stories and legends of how some humans battled the Mermaids while other humans befriended Mermaids. One must wonder if the Mermaid stories of old are not somehow related to the Dogon god, Nommo, and the Babylonia god, Oannes.

Conclusion: I have always loved history, but as with most folks I assumed that the history I was taught in school was the whole truth. In college, I minored in history, but only the history of the United States extending back two to three hundred years. I knew very little about ancient history until I accepted the reality that I was an alien abductee. This reality compelled me to search for answers, and I soon learned that my answers would not come unless I delved back into human history as far as I could go. The study of ancient cultures is where I needed to begin and to focus on the ancient gods of their religious beliefs. I also felt that I needed to have a very "open mind" because my modern day beliefs were about to be put to the test. This part was not going to be easy. At this period of my life, I had just recently bolted from the denomination that I had participated in my whole life and was struggling with my religious beliefs that I was a sinner for leaving the church.

Grudgingly, I moved forward down an unknown path with thoughts of "going to hell" dancing in my thoughts, but as fate would have it, it was the path I was destined to travel and that I am still travelling today. I have met wonderful friends along this path and have become good friends with many. The main key to these friendships was respect for different beliefs. By doing so, I have opened myself up to learn new answers to the many questions I have. These answers have allowed me to formulate theories about the "Alien Agenda" as it pertains to me.

There seems to be no doubt that more than one species of ET's are interacting with humans and have been doing so for a long, long time. As with human nature, there seem to be good ET's and bad ET's. I am experiencing this interaction for the most part with two species, "The Greys," and "The Reptilians."

The Grey's agenda for me seems to revolve around them learning my emotions. I believe the reason behind this is that they have evolved to a point where their technology has basically eliminated the majority of their emotions to such a degree that they do not have enough emotions to keep in check their advanced technology. As in the ying-yang; something cannot exist without an opposite. How as humans would we know how sweet the taste of sugar is if there were not something sour to judge it by. There is nothing wrong with technology, but when technology begins to overshadow the emotions in an intelligent species, then over time the intelligent species will die out. To counter the lack of emotions which is helping to destroy their species, the Greys are trying to learn human emotions to instill emotions into a new species of Greys...The Hybrids. In this way, through the original Grey species will eventually die off, the Grey Hybrids will emerge as a new and better Grey species.

Now with the Reptilian agenda, I am more reluctant to share my theories because it goes against all that is considered rational, logical thinking and status-quo religious beliefs, but I will. After looking back in history, I cannot help but wonder if these ancient gods were in fact different ET species with a specific agenda based on if they were good ETs or bad ETs. My personal theory is that the Reptilians began as benefactors toward human evolution, but somewhere down the line their agenda changed. Maybe it was the god-like worship bestowed upon the Reptilian by humans that super charged their ego. Maybe through the years they manipulated the genetic code of humans trying to make a better or different human for unknown reasons. I cannot pass up on the theory that maybe these ETs came down to earth before intelligent life even existed on earth and took existing life forms and created humans. Scientists are still looking for the "Missing Link" on the human tree of life.

Before writing these theories off to some delusional thinking, one need only look at what human scientists are accomplishing in the lab today. Dolly the sheep is supposedly the perfect clone given birth by scientists manipulating the cells of another sheep. There is serious talk of cloning a human, and some believe that this has already been done and soon having the technology to create the perfect, designer baby. When I hear of this, I looked at the alien species grabbing me for their physical, emotional and mental experiments and can see our technology moving forward on the same path as alien technology. As I have shared many times before, if you see one alien of a certain species, then you see them all. There is no doubt in my mind what-so-ever that each alien is a clone of another alien. By having the technology to clone your species, you are eliminating the one basic fundamental emotional need in an intelligent species to procreate, and if one falls, then others are sure to follow.

There is one more agenda theory of mine that I would like to share. There are few things that I write down in stone that I know to be the truth about aliens. These few things are these: I am an alien abductee. I have been one since I was a small child. My abductions are ongoing to my current age of 61. I do not like the abduction because they take me against my free will. Other than these few things most of what I share are theories, ideas and opinions, but there is one more thing that I am pretty sure that is occurring.

I believe that a part of our government, military and intelligence agencies know without a doubt that ET's are coming to earth, interacting and abducting humans. I believe that sometime in the past there was an agreement signed or agreed to by humans with at least several of these ET species. I believe that part of this agreement allows ET's to interact with and abduct humans with no interference from any government on earth in exchange for advanced ET technology. I am not the only one who believes this, and there is some very good evidence to support this claim.

Now in closing, I suggest that others who are looking for their answers, their truth follow the advice of a preacher at the end of his Sunday Sermon:

Listen, look, learn, but make up your own mind.

# From the Author

As you can tell from reading the views, theories and opinions of these very knowledgeable UFO researchers who have so graciously contributed to this book, there is no one answer that satisfies the question of what the alien agenda might be. The subject itself is much too vast and complex for a simple easy explanation. I personally believe that the alien agenda lies in direct correlation to the specific needs of that particular race of extraterrestrial beings. Those needs may sometime overlap with other alien races, and they may indeed work together to achieve their predetermined objectives. It is also quite probable that at least one and quite possibly several of these alien visitors to our blue planet are working with various governments, or secret divisions of such, in a trade for certain technology used and known by the aliens. There has been a vast amount of evidence presented over the years that would lean heavily toward validation of this belief especially in the case of the Greys and the alien species commonly referred to as the Reptilians, which are large lizard like alien creatures widely believed to dwell in underground tunnels and facilities while here on earth.

Although I would like to concur with the popular mainstream thought that all extraterrestrial creatures visiting us are kind beings, our "space brothers" if you will, only here to help mankind, I unequivocally cannot! I am not implying that all aliens are malevolent; however, I do believe there is that element of alien species here. In my experience with the Greys, I would say they have demonstrated both benevolent and malevolent behavior. They have performed tortuous, cruel acts upon me and yet they have also healed me which is in and of itself a contradiction. Of course, there is always the possibility that I was only healed because they needed me healthy for their own uses, not out of any act of kindness on their part.

My experiences with the Greys have persisted for decades now and over the years I have learned much about this particular species of alien beings. Through it all, I still cannot say definitively whether or not what I believe to be the Greys agenda is actually their true agenda. I can only take the accumulation of my numerous abduction experiences and speculate what that agenda might be based on what I've witnessed and experienced. The Greys are creating a new species, hybrids; a race of beings that is a mix of human DNA and their own.

Even with all of our faults and genetic flaws, humans seem to have certain qualities that the Greys seek and desire within themselves. Perhaps these are long lost traits that their kind once had, and they now have an urgent need to obtain them again and implement them back into the evolution of their species. It's almost as if they are now experiencing a form of de-evolution instead of the natural progression of an improved evolution a species needs in order to continue to survive. There are several traits among our own species that I believe the Greys are most interested in. The first is quite simply, our bodies. Humans are larger, stronger, quicker and more agile than the small thin and fragile Greys are. Maybe at one time in their ancestral history they too had bodies more closely resembling humans. Perhaps they lost the need for muscle and size over generations as they used and relied more on their brain power and technology. I can only theorize as to the reasons behind the Greys fascination with the human body.

As I have previously written in earlier chapters of this book, the Grey aliens appear to me to be completely devoid of emotions. This is especially true of the small worker Greys; they act and work in a very matter of fact manner. I believe that there is a strong possibility that the small Greys are some sort of biological robot. I know that this notion is far beyond our current comprehension and scientific abilities but their actions and mannerisms suggest to me that it could be real. They have no emotion other than something that is contrived for a purpose. They seem to exhibit what I would describe as a hive mentality. Their thought process is based entirely on logic. When something happens that isn't logical they appear to get confused as if they aren't programmed to understand what to do or how to react. The tall Greys do not act like the smaller ones. They will have a conversation with you and at times, even answer some questions. They are clearly in charge. Their thinking process, mannerisms and actions are different than the smaller Greys. It would not surprise me in the least bit to someday learn that the tall Greys created these smaller versions of themselves to use as workers.

I know one thing for sure; the Greys are very interested in human emotions. Many of the experiments done on me were based around monitoring and measuring my emotional reaction to certain situations that they would create and place me in. It could very well be that they use implants in humans as not only a tracking device but also as a way to monitor our emotions as we live our everyday life and go through the wide array of emotions that our life experiences bring upon us. Some alien abduction researchers believe that the Greys have such control over us that they can and do alter our feelings and emotions to the extent that they will bring certain individuals together either for predetermined genetics that they are looking for in a fetus that couple would create or to measure the emotions of those people together who have the genetic code they favor. This could also work in reverse, and when they decide to control our feelings and emotions about someone to the point of separating a couple when they no longer need one of the partners. I know the mind control abilities of these beings. It is impossible to explain how powerful it is. We are completely defenseless against this ability. One can talk all they want about weapons, but to me the mind is the most powerful weapon. This is something the Greys know and use masterfully.

It could very well be that they are going to such an extent as to bring certain people together and/or break them apart. It is certainly within the realm of possibility for them. I think that they need to understand the emotional aspect of the human psyche in order to understand the new breed of hybrids that they are creating since this genetic trait is now in them to some extent. Not only does it help them with the hybrids but it also helps them with their interaction with humans. Through leaning about our emotions and what kind of situation will set off what emotion they learn what to expect from us. What to do for what they want to achieve. Another important reason for them to have so much interest in human emotions has to do with their immense interest in human sexuality.

This interest seems to go far beyond the science of how humans reproduce. I'm sure they figured that out rather quickly. They want to know what causes human sexual desire. They want to learn why some of us are attracted to each other or sexually aroused by a certain act and someone else might not be. I don't think they fully understand what attracts us to each other or the whole concept of desire. Why someone might find something attractive in another person and some else doesn't. They are fascinated by the whole idea of sex between us and everything that it encompasses. Many of their experiments on humans are based around this very concept. I have personally witnessed them and have been forced into being a participant. No matter what sort of sexual scenario they subject you to, they are always there watching, monitoring, and observing with an intense interest. Most of the time there will be several aliens conducting and watching while these sexually induced experiments take place. They usually will make no effort to conceal their presence while they are observing. Not only are abductees forced into sexual acts with other abductees but many, including me, are forced into intercourse with the female alien hybrids. I wrote about this event in an earlier chapter. I don't remember if that is what happened although I'm sure that was the intent, so it probably did.

I would like to reiterate that no one that is a part of any of these sexual escapades conducted by the Greys are willing participants. It is demeaning and nothing short of being a sex slave. If they want your sperm, they are going to take it. If they want you to have sex with other humans who are complete strangers to you, then that is what is going to happen. If they want you to have sex with one of their female hybrids, you will. What you want or don't want to do is of no consequence to the Greys. The mental power and control these alien beings have over us humans is beyond what most of our planets inhabitants can comprehend. Unless you have experienced that kind of mental suppression and forced submission through it, you will never fully understand the magnitude of what alien abductees have to endure.

The Greys get what they want. The do what they need to do in order to achieve and complete their objective. Maybe they don't have any choice but to do some of the sadistic and heinous acts on us that they do. Maybe they aren't that much different than us in that regard. They do what is necessary in order for their species to survive just as we do. Having been a part of the Greys agenda and subjected to so many procedures and experiments executed by them, I would like to believe that an advanced civilization such as they are have no choice but to do what they do to us in order to continue to survive. Holding on to the belief gives me at least some degree of comfort knowing that everything I've went through all these years had a valid reason behind it. It also gives me hope for the human race in that evolution will eventually weed out our violent nature, our hate for each other, our disrespect for nature and our planet, our war like mentality and greed. Would we be like the Greys and only do what is necessary to the hapless victims we captured or would we get what we needed from them and then kill them only to go looking for the next victim? One only need visit any of the thousands of laboratories around the world where testing and experiments are routinely done on animal species less intelligent than us to get the answer to that question.

The number of planets with the possibility of intelligent life is overwhelming. New ones are being discovered on a regular basis these days. Many of these planets are billions of years older than Earth. It is difficult for us to imagine the technology that any intelligent life form from any such planet would possess or just how superior to us the intelligence of that life form would be. We have reached a stage in our evolution that it is time for mankind to set aside it's ego and the belief that we are alone in the universe. Science, quantum physics, and the multitudes of eye witnesses and experiencers around the globe are now telling us that we are not. Ancient civilizations from our own past left us message after message telling us the same for those willing to accept it. Whatever agenda these other advance extraterrestrial beings had or continue to have is not known with any certainty. The Greys agenda is what it is; for whatever reason they need to create a hybrid species. I wish I wasn't a part of it, but I am. There is nothing I can do about it but accept it and do my best to understand the rationale behind it. As for my experiences with them, the agenda continues. The mission on earth for the Greys is not complete. Will the children of the Greys continue this mission? Only time will tell.

# Works Cited List:

http://andromida.hubpages.com/hub/annunaki

www.wikipedia.com

Vallee, Jacques. Dimensions: A Casebook of Alien Contact. USA: Anomalist Books, 2008

Sutherland, Mary. In Search of Shambhala. USA: We-Publish, 2003

Made in the USA
Lexington, KY
11 August 2018